" .. present your bodies
A LIVING SACRIFICE..."

Romans 12:1

Basic Lesson Series—Volume 1

A LIVING SACRIFICE

"Exercise thyself unto godliness"
1 Timothy 4:7

Watchman Nee

Christian Fellowship Publishers, Inc.
New York

Available from the Publishers at:
11515 Allecingie Parkway
Richmond, Virginia 23235

Basic Lessons—Volume 1

CONTENTS

BASIC LESSONS
ON
PRACTICAL CHRISTIAN LIVING

Burdened with the need of a firm foundation for the Christian life, brother Watchman Nee gave a series of basic lessons on practical Christian living during the training session for workers held in Kuling, Foochow, China in 1948. He expressed the hope that these essential lessons might be faithfully learned by God's people, thereby laying a good foundation for the building up of the Body of Christ.

These messages on practical Christian living have now been translated from the Chinese language and will be published in a series of six books, bearing the various titles of: (1) *A Living Sacrifice*; (2) *The Good Confession*; (3) *Assembling Together*; (4) *Not I, But Christ*; (5) *Do All to the Glory of God*; and (6) *Love One Another*.

"Exercise thyself unto godliness" (I Tim. 4:7), is the exhortation of the apostle Paul. May our hearts be so exercised by God's Word as to give the Holy Spirit opportunity to perfect the new creation.

All quotations of the Scriptures, unless otherwise indicated, are from the American Standard Version of the Bible (1901).

LESSON ONE

BAPTISM

Realizing the comprehensiveness of baptism in the Bible, we shall focus our consideration on just two of its aspects which, we are convinced, every new believer must know. These two aspects are: (1) What can baptism do for a person? and (2) What is the real meaning of baptism? Before the believer is baptized, he should look ahead and ask: Now that I am going into the water, what will baptism do for me? This is viewing baptism in advance. But after baptism, the believer needs to cast a backward look and ask the second question: What is the meaning of this which I have undergone? The first is foresight, an understanding before baptism; the second is hindsight, an ascertaining following baptism.

Two Sets of Scriptures On Baptism

Set 1:
He that believeth and is baptized shall be saved; but he that disbelieveth shall be condemned.

Mk. 16:16

1

And Peter said unto them, Repent ye, and be baptized every one of you in the name of Jesus Christ unto the remission of your sins; and ye shall receive the gift of the Holy Spirit.

Acts 2:38

And now why tarriest thou? arise, and be baptized, and wash away thy sins, calling on his name.

Acts 22:16

That aforetime were disobedient, when the longsuffering of God waited in the days of Noah, while the ark was a preparing, wherein few, that is, eight souls, were saved through water: which also after a true likeness doth now save you, *even* baptism, not the putting away of the filth of the flesh, but the interrogation of a good conscience toward God, through the resurrection of Jesus Christ.

I Pet. 3:20–21

Set 2:
Or are ye ignorant that all we who were baptized into Christ Jesus were baptized into his death? We were buried therefore with him through baptism into death: that like as Christ was raised from the dead through the glory of the Father, so we also might walk in newness of life.

Rom. 6:3–4

Having been buried with him in baptism, wherein ye were also raised with him through faith in the working of God, who raised him from the dead.

Col. 2:12

The first set of Scriptures above is concerned with what baptism will do to the one baptized, while the second set

2

explains the meaning of baptism. The one deals with what the believer ought to know on this side of the water, that is, in advance of baptism; the other treats of what he should know on the farther side of the water, after baptism. Let us look at these respectively.

What Can Baptism Do for a Person?

"He that believeth and is baptized shall be saved; but he that disbelieveth shall be condemned."

Mk. 16:16

1. SHALL BE SAVED.

We would suppose that most Protestants become a bit apprehensive over this verse. When they see it, they change it in their mind to read "He *that believeth* and *is* saved shall be baptized." The Lord, however, has not so said. In order to escape the error of the Roman Catholic Church, Protestants unwittingly alter God's Word and thus fall into another error. The Lord speaks clearly that "he that believeth and is baptized shall be saved." No one is authorized to change it to "he that believeth and is saved shall be baptized."

THE OBJECTIVE OF SALVATION IS THE WORLD

Now let us be clear as to the meaning of the word "salvation" in the Bible. What is the objective of salvation? This may not be easily understood by new believers because they lack an accurate knowledge of what salvation is. According to the Bible, salvation is related to the world, not to hell. The opposite of eternal life is perdition, while the opposite of salvation is the world. We are to be saved out of the world. As long as we belong to the world, we are in the state of perdition.

It is imperative for us to understand man's state before God. People of the world today need not do anything to cause them to perish. No one is required to kill in order to perish; nor by not killing will any be spared from perdition. The whole world is perishing, but God is pulling out some from among the perishing. So far as the whole world is concerned, it is already damned; but so far as individuals are concerned, this one and that one are being saved. It is not separating a flock of one hundred into fifty sheep and fifty goats; rather, it is netting some fish out of a sea of fish. All those that are caught in the net are saved while those that remain in the sea are yet lost.

Therefore, in answering the question of whether one is saved or lost, the issue does not rest on one's personal conduct; it is instead settled by the person's whereabouts. If he is in the boat, he is saved; if he is still in the sea, he is lost. It makes no difference if one is good or bad, a gentleman or a villain, with or without conscience. As long as he is in the world, he is lost. If he has not come out, has not left that place which is under judgment, he is a condemned sinner.

SALVATION IS A MATTER OF POSITION

"For as through the one man's disobedience (Adam's) the many were made sinners" (Rom. 5:19). It is not necessary for a person to sin in order to be qualified as a sinner. Because of one man's sin, all have been constituted sinners. As long as the person is in Adam, that is, in the world, he stands opposite to God, and is therefore an enemy of God. His position is wrong, for it is a lost position. This, then, is the story of the unsaved.

4

Brethren, let us be absolutely clear as to the real meaning of "salvation." It is a word frequently used but used with such confusion. So far as today is concerned, eternal life is not as broad in its scope as salvation, for to have eternal life is today a personal matter. But to be saved indicates both a coming out of a particular brotherhood as well as a receiving of eternal life. Hence to have eternal life is purely personal while to be saved is personal plus corporate.

Salvation speaks of my leaving one brotherhood, and entering into another. Eternal life merely tells me what I have entered into, but it leaves unmentioned from where I came. Salvation includes the coming out as well as the entering in, whereas eternal life simply deals with the entering in. As a result, during this present age salvation is more comprehensive in its scope than eternal life, for it deals with the matter of being delivered from the world, of coming out of the world.

Let us notice the four cardinal facts concerning the world as shown in the Bible: (a) The world is condemned or judged before God, (b) the world lies in the evil one, (c) the world crucified the Lord Jesus, and (d) the world is an enemy to God. Please note that the world not only sins, but crucified the Lord Jesus as well. It is therefore God's enemy. These are the four cardinal facts of the world as God sees it. All who are in the world, irrespective of their personal conduct, are already judged and thus in perdition.

What is wrong with people in this world is far more than personal unrighteous acts of behavior. Their very position is wrong before God. How can a person forsake the world if he is still keenly aware of its loveliness? But one day he is made to see the wrong position of the world be-

5

fore God. However lovely the world may be, it has to be forsaken. So salvation deals with deliverance from an improper relationship with and position in the world.

The Jewish people once cried out, "His blood be on us, and on our children" (Matt. 27:25). Although I am not directly responsible for the slaying of the Lord Jesus, my forefathers did murder Him. Even though I am not personally engaged in the act, yet I belong to that brotherhood which has slain the Lord. The brotherhood I am with is God's enemy and it is condemned. Whether I myself am right or wrong is another question. What lies before me is this: I need God to enlighten me that I may see that the brotherhood to which I belong is wrong. The world I am in is wrong in that it has killed the Lord Jesus and is therefore constituted God's enemy. It is already judged by God. I need to be released from such a relationship; I need to be delivered from that position.

What is meant by salvation then? To be saved is to be released from that brotherhood, that position, and that relationship to the world. In other words, I come out of the world. People are usually most concerned with their personal justification, but they need to be reminded of the place from which they have been saved. Salvation is to be saved out of the world, not merely out of hell, for the world is under the judgment of God.

BAPTISM FOLLOWS BELIEVING

There is not the slightest doubt that whosoever believes in the Lord Jesus has eternal life. We have preached this glad news for many years. As soon as one believes in the Lord Jesus, whoever he may be, he receives eternal life and is thereby forever favored by God. But let us remember: believing without being baptized is not yet salvation.

6

Indeed, you have believed; indeed, you have eternal life; but you are not yet reckoned as a saved person in the eyes of the world. As long as you are not baptized, you will not be recognized as saved. Why? Because no one knows your difference from the rest of the world. You must rise up and be baptized, declaring the termination of your relationship with the world; then and only then are you saved.

What is baptism? It is your emancipation from the world. It frees you from the brotherhood to which you once belonged. The world knew that you were one with it, but the moment you are baptized, it immediately becomes aware of the fact that you are finished with it. The friendship which you had maintained so many years has now come to an end. You were buried in the tomb, you terminated your course in the world. Before baptism, you knew you had eternal life; after baptism, you know you are saved. Everybody recognizes that you are the Lord's, for you belong to Him.

"He that believeth and is baptized shall be saved." Why? Because having believed and been baptized, it is now an open fact where one stands. Were there no faith, there would not be that inward fact which alone makes things real. But with that inward reality, baptism puts one outside of the world and terminates the former relationship with the world. Baptism, therefore, is separation.

NO BAPTISM, NO TESTIMONY

"But he that disbelieveth shall be condemned." Disbelief alone is enough for condemnation. As long as one belongs to the world brotherhood, his disbelief seals his condemnation. In contrast, he who believes must be baptized, for as long as he is not baptized, he has not come out of the world in outward testimony.

We discover three amazing facts in the religious world of Judaism, Hinduism and Islamism.

(a) Judaism persecutes the baptized. Among the Jews, a person may be a secret Christian without being persecuted. The greatest difficulty with many hundreds and thousands of Jews is not in believing the Lord Jesus but rather in being baptized. Once the person is baptized he is liable to be cast out and disowned.

(b) Hinduism ostracizes the baptized. In India, no one will lay hands on you if you remain unbaptized. But as soon as you *are* baptized, you will be ostracized. It is as if the world permits you to have eternal life but stands against anyone being baptized.

(c) Islamism murders the baptized. The reaction of Islamism is more severe. It is rare to find a living Mohammedan who has turned Christian, for the Moslems kill those that do. One of the most successful workers among the Mohammedans, Dr. Zwemer, once declared that his work would never be big since the results of his labor all ended in death; no one lived on. Among the Mohammedans, those who believe must immediately be sent away or else within two or three days after baptism they will be murdered.

Baptism is a public announcement that declares, "I have come out of the world." Never take the word "salvation" purely in the personal sense. According to the Bible, it is more a matter of coming out of the world than of escaping hell.

2. UNTO THE REMISSION OF SINS.

"And Peter said unto them, Repent ye, and be baptized every one of you in the name of Jesus Christ unto the remission of your sins" (Acts 2:38). Does the word of the apostle sound strange in our ears? Again, many Protestants seem to have difficulty with this verse so plainly spoken by the apostle. In what way can baptism lead to the forgiveness of sins? Is it not strange that the apostle does not lay stress on "believing" in his message?

We may ask ourselves whether Peter in this message recorded in Acts 2 is seeking to persuade people to believe. Not at all. Is this a reflection upon Peter's ability to preach the gospel? Is his preaching inferior to ours? Is his presentation inadequate? We know that, according to the whole Bible, the most important point touching the gospel is belief. How then is it that Peter overlooks such a cardinal feature? He can omit other less important aspects but surely not this one. Yet strangely enough, he speaks on baptism instead of on faith, and the Holy Spirit causes a pricking of the hearts of those who listen to him. In accordance with orthodoxy, we would claim that faith alone is necessary; but Peter declares that his hearers must be baptized in the name of Jesus Christ.

Why is it that Peter speaks only of baptism? It is because all of his hearers were participants in the killing of the Lord Jesus. Fifty days ago they had cried out: "Away with this man!" (Luke 23:18) They had been in the crowd shouting their rejection. Now, though, some of them desired to be separated from the crowd. How? By being baptized. Through baptism they would come out of the world and sever their relationship with that brotherhood. As soon as I step into the water to be baptized, my sins are remitted, that is, I come out of the brotherhood to which I once belonged. This is why Peter on Pentecost tells them to be baptized in the name of the Lord Jesus that their sins may be remitted. This single act of baptism causes them to come out of the world.

9

Do you now see that you who originally were of the world and therefore were enemies of the Lord will be saved if you come out of it? You need to confess before God and man that you have come out and are today no longer associated with the world. This is the greatest teaching of Pentecost. Let our minds be molded by God's record instead of by any system of Protestant theology.

3. Wash Away Sins.

Let us next consider the case of Paul. Ananias says to Paul, "Arise, and be baptized, and wash away thy sins, calling on his name" (Acts 22:16).

Paul is universally accepted as the foremost teacher and prophet and apostle in Christianity. What if there were some flaw in his experience as well as in his teaching? He is told not to tarry but to arise and be baptized. Why? To wash away his sins. The Roman Catholic Church errs here in changing this verse into a personal experience before God. They fail to see that this Scripture deals with the question of the world. Consequently they baptize dying people in order to wash away their sins. They do not recognize that baptism is related to the world instead of to God. But Protestants equally err in attempting to hide the verse.

Being formerly a person of the world, Paul, now that he has both believed and seen the Lord Jesus, should arise and be baptized. Thus baptized, his sins are washed away, for he has severed his relationship with the world. If one becomes a Christian secretly without being baptized, the world will still consider him one of its own. The believer may say he is saved, but the world will not accept his statement. Not until he is baptized does he compel the world to see his salvation. Who would be so foolish as to go into the water unless there were a good reason for it? Yes, as soon as a Christian is baptized he is freed from the world. Hence this water is linked to the world.

The world will still reckon a person one of its own if he does not give an outward expression of his inward faith. For example, in Kuling, Foochow, there is an idol festival in the autumn. Every inhabitant is supposed to contribute to it. If one merely says he has believed in the Lord and cannot therefore participate, he will nonetheless not be excused. But let him be baptized, and he will immediately be known as having left the world. Consequently, baptism is the best way of separation. Through baptism the believer declares to the entire world that he has severed his relationship with it and has come out of it.

Since baptism is a public testimony, it should be openly conducted. Oftentimes unbelievers may come to a baptismal service. But some believers suggest that in order to avoid confusion there should not be too many spectators in a baptismal service. Well then, does this mean that John the Baptist has yet something to learn at *their* feet, for without doubt the scene at the Jordan River was quite disorganized! No, let the world witness what we are doing!

4. Saved Through Water.

God's words maintain a unity of thought. It is said in 1 Peter 3:20–21 ". . . in the days of Noah . . . wherein few, that is, eight souls, were saved through water." This gives a slightly different angle to salvation. The Lord states that "he that believeth and is baptized shall be saved"; Peter declares on the Day of Pentecost, "Repent ye, and be baptized every one of you in the name of Jesus Christ unto the remission of your sins; and ye shall receive the gift of the Holy Spirit"; Paul is told to "arise and be baptized,

and wash away (his) sins, calling on his (Christ's) name";
but Peter here shows us how to be saved through ("dia" in
the original) water.

Whatever cannot pass through water is not saved but is
drowned. At the time of Noah all were baptized, but only
eight souls came safely out of the water. Except for the
eight, all were washed down and failed to come up. In
other words, to them the water became the water of death.
But to us, this water is the water of salvation. They were
immersed by the water and sank to the bottom, but we
emerged from it. Do you not notice that there is something
positive in Peter's word? It is quite true that when the
flood came, all mankind was drowned. There were nevertheless eight persons in the ark who emerged from the
water. The water could not retain them. These eight were
saved while the remainder all perished. Today the whole
world lies under the wrath of God. Yet if I am baptized, I
have passed through God's wrath and have come out from
the condemned world. This is the meaning of baptism.

Baptism is immersion on the one side and emergence on
the other side. It speaks of passing through the water and
of coming out of it. Let us emphasize the side of emergence. All went into the water, but only eight persons
came out. Today we too are saved by baptism. How is
this? Because we have entered into the water and have
then emerged from it. No person who has not yet believed
in the Lord Jesus should be baptized, for he will not be
able to emerge from the water. But we believers can testify
to the world that we have found the way out.

HEREAFTER WE ARE OUT OF THE WORLD

From this first set of four Scripture passages, we now
ought to be clear as to what baptism can do for us. As we

12

are baptized, we are delivered from the world. The new believer should not let many years pass before he is liberated from the world. The first thing he should do is be baptized. He must understand what the state of the world is before God. What is it to be saved? It is to be dissociated from one's former state. It is to have one's relationship with the world cleanly dissolved. Henceforth the believer is on the other side of the world. The newly converted needs to be shown this way.

Soon after one has believed in the Lord, he should be shown that he is one who stands outside the world. His baptism is a definite expression of his being delivered from the world. Hereafter he abides in the ark and therefore has gone over to the other side. Many things he cannot do, not only for the sake of his having believed in the Lord Jesus but also because of his having been baptized. He has crossed over a bridge to the other side. This makes baptism most meaningful.

BAPTISM MEANS YOU ARE FINISHED

The error of Protestantism is in overlooking the significance of baptism when it seeks to perfect the doctrine of salvation. We must restore the place of baptism today. What is its meaning? It is a coming out of the world; it is the proper procedure for being delivered from the world. When one is baptized he declares to people that he has come out of the world. Miss M. E. Barber has put it in poetic form: "Then the grave, with dear ones weeping, knowing that all life has fled." These dear ones know that you are finished, that you have come to the end of your road. Such baptism is most effective. Anything higher than this would be impractical. You must come out of the old realm. To have eternal life is the story of your spirit before

God; but to be saved is your testimony to the world by declaring you no longer have any part in it.

What Is the Real Meaning of Baptism?

Now that the Christian is baptized, he needs to look back and assess the real meaning of baptism. "Or are ye ignorant that all we who were baptized into Christ Jesus were baptized into his death?" (Rom. 6:3). "Having been buried with him in baptism, wherein ye were also raised with him through faith in the working of God, who raised him from the dead" (Col. 2:12). This is a looking backward, not forward. Remember that the words in Mark 16, Acts 2, Acts 22, and 1 Peter 3 were words spoken *before* baptism, while the words in Romans 6 and Colossians 2 were spoken *after* baptism. After baptism, we are notified by God that in our baptism we were actually baptized into the Lord's death and were buried with Him, and so also we were raised with Him in resurrection.

Romans 6 stresses death and burial, though in addition it touches upon resurrection. Colossians 2, however, emphasizes burial and resurrection. It is therefore a step further, for its focal point is resurrection. The water serves as a tomb. What is buried must be dead, but what emerges must be alive in resurrection. Romans describes the first part of the truth and Colossians the last part of the same truth.

1. So Great A Gospel

Perhaps one time when you sensed the heaviness of your sins, you heard of the death of the Lord Jesus. Such news was truly the gospel to you. Or, perhaps at a time when you were conscious of how wicked you are and, tried your best to free yourself from the dominion of sin and yet couldn't—perhaps at that time you learned that you were already dead. That indeed was the gospel to you. Praise be to God, for such is the gospel of Jesus Christ. As the death of the Lord is a great gospel, so our death in Christ is also a great gospel. It is a joyous thing to know of the Lord's death; it is equally joyous to know of one's own death in the Lord. What is your first thought upon hearing of the news of death? Like Joseph of Arimathea, you think of burial, for burial is the first human reaction to death. The gospel proclaims today that you are dead in Christ. The first thing to do thereafter is to prepare for burial.

Therefore, beloved, when you step into the water of baptism or when you look back to your baptism after the lapse of many years, you need to remember that you are one already dead. You ask people to bury you because you believe you are dead. You would no doubt vigorously object if anyone should want to bury you before your death. Even if you were too weak to voice your objection, you would certainly resist being buried before you had breathed your last breath. Death is therefore *the* prerequisite of burial.

New believers should be instructed that at the time of the crucifixion of the Lord Jesus they too were crucified. It is on this basis that they request to be buried in water. But just as the Lord Jesus was raised from among the dead, they too shall be raised through the working of the same power of resurrection within them. In coming out of the water, they become resurrected ones; they are no longer their former selves.

This is something which they ought often to look back upon. Having believed that they were dead, they asked to be buried. Now having emerged from the water, they thus shall walk in newness of life. They are now on the resurrection side.

2. WE ARE IN CHRIST

Once there was a heading in a newspaper which read: "One Person, Three Lives." The story was this: after a pregnant woman had been murdered, the medical authorities subsequently discovered that there were twins in her womb. Hence, the peculiar headline! May we draw your attention to the fact that in the case of our Lord, it is one Person but countless lives. This is actually the meaning of the scriptural phrase, "in Christ." Outwardly the murderer killed only the mother, but since twins were in the mother's womb, they too died when the mother died. Likewise, this happens to those who are in Christ. When Christ died, we too died.

"But of him (God) are ye in Christ Jesus" (1 Cor. 1:30). It is of God that we are in Christ, and the fact is we *are* in Christ. Since one died, we all died. Were we ignorant of the meaning of being in Christ, we could never understand what co-death with Him is. The twins could die, together with the mother, because they were in the mother's womb. Spiritual truth is even more real than physical fact. God has joined us to Christ, hence His death is our death.

We have already died in Christ. Let us believe this fact. In being immersed in and emerging from the water, we declare that we are on the other side of the tomb. This is resurrection. The reckoning in Romans 6 is to reckon to our being alive to God in Christ Jesus as well as to our being dead to sin in Christ Jesus. Though in ourselves we may not feel any difference, yet this glorious experience is in Christ.

16

We sincerely hope that all new believers will be brought into this exercise. In realizing they are dead, they allow themselves to be buried in water. By seeing they are resurrected, they come out of the water to serve God.

CONCLUDING THE PAST

After one believes in the Lord, he invariably has a number of things from the past that await termination. The question before us is: how should he conclude them?

The Teaching of the Bible

In the Bible, especially in the New Testament, God does not seem to stress much on the things which one did before he trusted in the Lord. Try to find some passages anywhere between Matthew and Revelation which deal with the concluding of the past. If you do try, you will have to concede that it is extremely difficult to find such passages. True, the epistles do recount our past improper manner of life; they also reveal to us what our future actions should be. But they do not recommend what to do about our past. For instance, in both the letter to the Ephesians and that to the Colossians our past is mentioned, but neither of them tells us how we ought to conclude it. They only deal with what we should do hereafter. The same is true in the letters to the Thessalonians. They too recall the past without specifying how to conclude it, for the emphasis again is on the future, as if the past were no longer a problem.

However, there is no doubt that the past needs to be properly concluded. Many revivalists preach relentlessly on the conclusion of the past by new believers. Can it be that they overstress this matter? In studying the word of God, it seems the apostles and even John the Baptist paid little attention to it.

1. THE ANSWERS OF JOHN THE BAPTIST

When the multitudes asked the question, "What then must we do?" John the Baptist, answering, said to them, "He that hath two coats, let him impart to him that hath none; and he that hath food, let him do likewise." You see, he referred not to the past but to the hereafter. And there also came publicans asking, "Teacher, what must we do?" He said to them, "Extort no more than that which is appointed you." And soldiers also asked him, saying "And we, what must we do?" And he said to them, "Extort from no man by violence, neither accuse any one wrongfully; and be content with your wages" (See Lk. 3:10–14). All these show us that even John, who preached repentance, did not stress the past but rather emphasized the future.

2. THE TEACHING OF PAUL

If we spend some time in perusing Paul's letters, we will find he always accentuates the hereafter, leaving the past unmentioned. Why? Because the past is all under the precious blood. A slight deviation in this matter would corrupt the gospel, pervert the teaching of repentance and even spoil the way of restitution. Hence, we must carefully, before God, solve this problem. It is true that there are certain things from the past which require an ending, but there are special reasons for these. We should be very clear as to our standing on this matter.

3. THE TEACHING OF FIRST CORINTHIANS

"Or know ye not that the unrighteous shall not inherit the kingdom of God? Be not deceived: neither fornicators, nor idolaters, nor adulterers, nor effeminate, nor abusers of themselves with men, nor thieves, nor covetous, nor drunkards, nor revilers, nor extortioners, shall inherit the kingdom of God. And such were some of you: but ye were washed, but ye were sanctified, but ye were justified in the name of the Lord Jesus Christ, and in the Spirit of our God" (I Cor. 6:9–11). Though Paul mentioned what the Corinthians were like and what they had done, yet he made no suggestion as how to solve those things. His emphasis on their being washed and sanctified and justified in the name of the Lord Jesus and in the Spirit of God surely was not directed toward the concluding of the past. Our Savior has already dealt with our past; hence, the point to stress today is on life from now on. One who is saved is washed, sanctified and justified.

4. THE TEACHING OF EPHESIANS

"And you did he make alive, when ye were dead through your trespasses and sins, wherein ye once walked according to the course of this world, according to the prince of the powers of the air, of the spirit that now worketh in the sons of disobedience; among whom we also all once lived in the lusts of our flesh, doing the desires of the flesh and of the mind, and were by nature children of wrath, even as the rest:—but God, being rich in mercy, for his great love wherewith he loved us, even when we were

21

dead through our trespasses, made us alive together with Christ" (Eph. 2:1–5). Nothing is taught here as to how we may best conclude all those things of the flesh, for the one all-inclusive conclusion is that our Lord, by the great love and rich mercy of God, has completely solved our past.

"This I say therefore, and testify in the Lord, that ye no longer walk as the Gentiles also walk, in the vanity of their mind, being darkened in their understanding, alienated from the life of God, because of the ignorance that is in them, because of the hardening of their heart; who being past feeling gave themselves up to lasciviousness, to work all uncleanness with greediness. . . . that ye put away, as concerning your former manner of life, the old man, that waxeth corrupt after the lusts of deceit; and that ye be renewed in the spirit of your mind, and put on the new man, that after God hath been created in righteousness and holiness of truth" (Eph. 4:17–24). These all pertain to the conditions of the past.

"Wherefore, putting away falsehood . . ." (Eph. 4:25a). Now he deals with the future. However, he only says to put away falsehood hereafter without telling how to deal with the past lies. "Speak ye truth each one with his neighbor . . . Be ye angry, and sin not: let not the sun go down upon your wrath: neither give place to the devil" (vv.25b–27). Nothing is said of the past but only of the future. "Let him that stole steal no more" (v.28a). Again the emphasis is on the hereafter; he does not deal with the problem of how to return what was stolen. "But rather let him labor, working with his hands the thing that is good . . . Let no corrupt speech proceed out of your mouth, but such as is good for edifying as the need may be, that it may give grace to them that hear. And grieve not the Holy Spirit of God . . . Let all bitterness, and wrath, and anger, and clamor, and railing, be put away from you, with all malice" (vv.28b—31). All these instructions follow the same tenor of touching only on one's life from now on.

"But fornication, and all uncleanness, or covetousness, let it not even be named among you, as becometh saints; nor filthiness, nor foolish talking, or jesting, which are not befitting: but rather giving of thanks" (Eph. 5:3–4). Still following the same principle, these words are related to the believer's conduct in the days to come, rather than to the concluding of the past during the time of unbelief.

From the epistles, we may discover a marvelous truth—what God stresses is the future of the believer. He is not concerned with the past life nor does He labor over what we should do about the past. This is a very basic understanding all believers need to have.

Due to some mistaken concepts of the gospel, dealing with the past is sometimes stressed to such an excess that it puts people into bondage. We are not suggesting that the past needs no dealing, for there are a few things which do require such dealing. However, we have to maintain that this is not foundational. God tells us that all our past sins are under the blood. We are completely forgiven because the Lord Jesus has died for us. We are saved through Christ our Substitute, not on the ground of our dealing with the past. No one is saved by his past good conduct, nor is anyone saved because of repentance for his past evil. We are saved through the redemption accomplished by the Lord Jesus on the cross. This alone is the foundation on which we firmly stand.

What Needs to be Dealt With

What, then, should we do about the past? After searching the New Testament carefully, we find a few places where this matter of concluding the past is mentioned. But all these cases are examples, none of them is a teaching. Our Lord has thus left us a few examples for our guidance in solving the past.

1. THINGS OF IDOLS MUST BE CONCLUDED

". . . turned unto God from idols" (I Thes. 1:9). Things pertaining to idols are not as simple as many think. Remember, we are the temple of the Holy Spirit. What agreement has the temple of God with idols? Even the apostle John, in writing to the believers, exhorts, "My little children, guard yourselves from idols" (I John 5:21).

We must understand the way Scripture views idolatry. God forbids the making of any graven image or any likeness of anything that is in heaven above or in the earth beneath or in the water; He also prohibits the entertaining of any thought that these images are alive. As soon as such a thought is cherished, these images become idols. The images in themselves are nothing, but if they are reckoned as alive, they turn diabolic. Hence the worship of these images is strictly forbidden; no heart is allowed to turn towards them. One of the ten commandments bans the making of images (see Deut. 5:8).

". . . Inquire not after their gods, saying, How do these nations serve their gods?" (Deut. 12:30b). Do not inquire after other gods through curiosity. Do not ask how the nations serve their gods. God forbids us to make such investigations for this will only lead to following the ways of the nations.

What agreement has the temple of God with idols? The application is clear: Christians are not to visit heathen temples except for special reasons, such as spending the night in the mountains where no other provision can be found.* They are not supposed to visit these temples for recreational purposes. It is not fitting for them to get too close to idols. "Guard yourselves from idols" means do not get too close to them.

"Nor take their names (other gods) upon my lips" (Ps. 16:4). Even in the pulpit we should be careful not to mention the names of other gods unless it is absolutely necessary for illustration. We should also put an end to all superstitions, not even entertaining any fear of fate. Too many believers still trust luck and pay attention to their fortunes as governed by their facial or palm configurations. Such things are prohibited. Whatever has anything at all to do with idolatry must be completely forfeited, once and for all, before God.

Starting from the very first day of his life of faith in Christ, a believer must be separated from idols and things pertaining to idolatry. He must not any more mention the names of idols, nor consult with fortunetellers. He should keep himself away from heathen temples, from entertaining any thought of worshipping images. He should not inquire into how other religions worship. The past must be totally concluded. Any idolatrous objects he may have should be smashed, not sold; they should be destroyed. This is very serious, for God is extremely jealous of idols.

If believers today are not wholly separated from idols, how can they escape the greatest idol of the future, even the image of anti-Christ? Not only that which is carved or molded should not be worshipped; likewise nothing living may be worshipped. The day is coming when the man of sin shall have a living image. No image can be wor-

* Editor's note: This was often true in China.

shipped, not even the so-called image of Christ or of Mary. The habit of not worshipping any image needs to be cultivated.

We must not serve in the flesh; we ought to serve in the spirit, for God is seeking for those who serve Him in spirit and not in flesh. God is a Spirit; He is not an image. Knowing this will deliver many believers from falling into the Roman Catholic Church, whose influence will greatly increase at the coming of the anti-Christ.

Hence, the first thing in concluding the past is to reject all former idols. We must turn from idols to wait for the Son of God at His second coming. We should not keep any image of the Lord Jesus; none is His true likeness and therefore is worthless. In the Vatican Museum there are over two thousand different images of the Lord Jesus. These are all the products of artists' imaginations. Many artists roam the world paying people to pose for them. Let us tell you, this is blasphemy. God is a jealous God, and He will not tolerate such a thing. All superstitions must be rejected; even every tinge of idolatry should be thoroughly cleared away.

2. CERTAIN THINGS REQUIRE A CONCLUSION

"And not a few of them that practised magical arts brought their books together and burned them in the sight of all: and they counted the price of them, and found it fifty thousand pieces of silver" (Acts 19:19). This, too, is something a new believer must bring to a conclusion. Though there is no command nor teaching, yet such dealing is clearly the result of the Holy Spirit's working. The Holy Spirit so works in believers that they bring forth those things which ought not to be in their possession and burn them. The books mentioned in Acts 19 were worth fifty thousand pieces of silver—a lot of money. But they were not sold so that the church might use the proceeds; rather they were burned. If Judas had been present, he certainly would have objected to that burning for the value of the books was worth far more than thirty pieces of silver; the money could have been used to aid the poor. The Lord, however, was pleased to have the books burned.

There are several things that need to be brought to a conclusion. Images are one, books on magic are another. The principle is clear: all images must be rejected and all doubtful things must be dealt with. We have the scriptural example that things that have a definite connection with sin, such as gambling instruments or obscene books, must be burned.

How about things which are unbecoming to the saints? In an unbeliever's home, it would be quite natural to find things connected with sin and things not befitting the saint. Thus, after one has believed in the Lord, he should go home and look over his belongings. Things connected with sin should be destroyed, not sold. Things unbefitting the saint may be altered where possible, as with clothing, or may be sold.

A good illustration is found in Leviticus 13 and 14 where it speaks of garments belonging to one who is leprous. Such garments may be likened to the things we need to deal with. Under investigation, some of those garments were found to have the plague of leprosy in them, and since they could not be washed they were burned with fire. Some garments, however, could be washed and the plague depart in the washing; these could be used again. In like manner, some of our clothes may be changed by shortening or lengthening them, for the problem involved is merely a matter of style. Others, however, are so involved with sin that they cannot be redeemed; therefore they must be burned.

A new believer needs to learn this lesson well at the outset, so that he will not be able to forget it throughout his life. He should be made to realize that to be a Christian is a very real thing. It involves much more than merely going to church and listening to sermons.

3. ALL INDEBTEDNESS MUST BE REIMBURSED

"And Zacchaeus stood, and said unto the Lord, Behold, Lord, the half of my goods I give to the poor; and if I have wrongfully exacted aught of any man, I restore fourfold" (Lk. 19:8). Zacchaeus sets us a good example. Strangely there is no teaching on this subject but each believer acts as he is moved by the Holy Spirit. Hence a little more here and a little less there, each doing as he is led by the Holy Spirit. If this were something merely of doctrine or teaching, then all would be done uniformly.

The power of the Lord was so strong upon Zacchaeus that he was willing to restore fourfold whatever he had wrongfully exacted from any man. Actually we would consider a twofold compensation as quite sufficient. The principle in Leviticus is to "add the fifth part more thereto" (Lev. 6:5). Suppose the indebtedness is a thousand dollars; then the reimbursement would be a thousand two hundred dollars. But when one is moved by the Holy Spirit, he must follow that moving, whether it be fourfold or even tenfold. Therefore, let us remember that the Bible does not give us any teaching on this matter; all that is given is simply the principle, the application of which is according to the leading of the Holy Spirit.

If a new believer has in the past extorted or cheated anybody or has stolen or taken possession of anything unrighteously, we believe he should deal with these things as the Lord works in him. Financially he may be unable to clear up what he has defrauded. Though this will not affect his being forgiven by God, it will have a definite bearing on his testimony.

For example: If I have stolen from a certain person a thousand dollars before I am saved, I cannot possibly preach the gospel to him if I have not cleared up that fraud. I may try to preach to him, but his mind most likely will only be occupied with that thousand dollars. No doubt I have been forgiven by God, but I have no testimony before that particular person. I cannot excuse myself from repaying him by saying, "Am I not forgiven by God?" This matter has much to do with my testimony.

Please remember: Zacchaeus returned fourfold for the sake of his testimony. At a time when people were all murmuring saying, "He (Jesus) is gone into lodge with a man that is a sinner," when they complained how much this man had extorted and wrongfully exacted of many, Zacchaeus stood and said, ". . . if I have wrongfully exacted aught of any man, I restore fourfold." This fourfold indemnity was not a condition for becoming a son of Abraham nor was it a requirement for receiving the salvation of God. But it was nonetheless the *result* of being a son of Abraham and the *result* of having salvation come to his house. His fourfold restoration sealed the mouths of his critics, for it was much more than he had defrauded. Due to this restoration of conduct, he had a testimony before men. This, then, is the ground for testimony.

I know a brother in the Lord who, before he was saved, was unrighteous in money matters and also sinful in certain conduct. He had many schoolmates, most of whom belonged to the upper middle class. After he was saved, he was quite zealous in trying to win his schoolmates to Christ, but he failed terribly. Though he earnestly preached the gospel to them, they could not believe him and wondered about his past fraud and misdemeanor. They had not forgotten his past, for he had never restored as Zacchaeus had done. His past sins were forgiven before God, but they remained a problem to men. Had he confessed his fault and paid back his debt, his testimony could have been received.

As a new believer, one needs to ask himself if he has wronged or defrauded anybody, if he has taken home things which do not belong to him or things which he has obtained unrighteously. If so, he could make a clean sweep of them by dealing with each one. Christian repentance includes the confession of past faults. It is not like ordinary repentance which simply involves a change of conduct. For example: if, as a worldling I often lost my temper in the past, it would be enough for me to show my repentance by not repeating it. But as a Christian, in addition to the change in conduct, I must also confess that losing my temper was wrong. I must not only control my temper before God but also I must confess to men my former fault of losing my temper. Thus shall this matter be concluded.

If one used to steal, he is clear now before God if he stops stealing. Yet this does not clear him before men. Even if for three consecutive years he steals nothing, men will still consider him as a thief. So, for the sake of testimony, not only must he stop stealing, but also he must confess to men his past fault. He is able to do this because he has been saved by grace.

A COMPLICATED PROBLEM

Here is a complicated problem: Suppose I have stolen ten thousand dollars, but now do not have even a thousand dollars with me. How then shall I solve this problem? In principle, I must confess candidly my fraud and concede that I am presently unable to repay. Reimbursement is one thing, confession is another thing. Whether or not I am capable of reimbursing, I must confess; otherwise I will never be able to testify. Although confession frequently means hardship, it still has to be done.

In the special situation of there having been killing involved, what should be done in order to conclude the past? The Bible records two such incidents, one in which the person is directly involved with the killing, the other in which he is indirectly involved. The first incident concerns the robber on the cross. The word "robber" in the Greek does not mean an ordinary robber but one who murders people, not a common thief but one who kills for money. But after this robber believed in the Lord, his sins were forgiven, for there is no sin which cannot be cleansed by the precious blood. The Lord said to him, "Verily I say unto thee, Today shalt thou be with me in Paradise" (Lk. 23:43). This robber did not deal with his past nor did he have the opportunity to do so. The Scripture mentions no more of his past, as if letting bygones be bygones. The second incident concerns Paul who was indirectly involved in a killing. He did not personally kill anybody, yet he was an accomplice in the murder of Stephen as he watched over the cloaks of those who stoned Stephen to death. Scripture, though, is just as silent on the dealing of the past in this case as in the former case.

In general principle, when we encounter such cases, we should not overburden the conscience of the new believer unless God especially works in his heart. In the two instances recorded in the New Testament, God seems to overlook the matter of restoring the past. Some believers, however, may not have peace in their conscience due to the working of the Holy Spirit within them. This is different from ordinary accusation. If they can express their regrets to the afflicted families, surely this is not something to be forbidden. Nevertheless, this is neither teaching nor commandment.

4. UNFINISHED THINGS MUST BE CONCLUDED

When a person becomes saved, he undoubtedly has many worldly affairs in his hands that are still unfinished. These may easily hamper his following the Lord. What is the scriptural way of concluding these things? When someone in the New Testament went to the Lord and said, "Lord, suffer me first to go and bury my father," the Lord Jesus answered him saying, "Follow me; and leave the dead to bury their own dead" (Matt. 8:21–22). So, in matters which are concerned with earthly responsibilities, the word of the Lord is: follow Me and let the dead bury the dead.

Here is an unbelieving father who is yet alive. The thought of the disciple is to go home and wait till his father is dead and buried before he comes to follow the Lord. But the Lord counteracts with the principle of letting the dead bury the dead. The first, "the dead," refers to the people of this world who are spiritually dead. The second, "the dead," refers to the physically dead. The Lord beckons him to follow and leave the burial to the worldlings. This is in no way to suggest to new believers that they should not perform filial and also funereal duties to their parents; rather, it is a principle on which to lay hold. Let the people of this world continue on with all the unfinished business. If we must finish these affairs ourselves, we may not have time to be Christians at all.

There is always the possibility the father will not die.

Hence we must let the dead bury the dead. This does not mean that we will not take care of things; it simply denotes that we will not allow such things to hinder us. Who can be a Christian if he must first take care of the thousand and one affairs of the family and of making a livelihood? Let us not wait until all these earthly affairs are taken care of before coming to Christ. If we do, we will never follow the Lord. Who would ever have the chance to believe the Lord if he had to finish all of his business first? Therefore, do not let these things of the dead bind us. To us, these things can be left unfinished. They can just be left behind as we start to follow the Lord.

From what we can find in the Word of God, these four items discussed above are the main things of the past which need to be concluded. A new believer should learn how to deal with each.

A Question

A question is raised: what if the person who has been wronged is not aware of it? Should such sin be confessed to him too?

The answer is: is there any physical indebtedness involved? If there is, it must be confessed. The best way to do this, though, is together with the church. For example: if I have caused you to incur a loss of a thousand dollars, I should be willing to confess this and reimburse you. But I must do it in the way that will be most profitable to you. A new believer tends to go to extremes and thus may spoil things. It is best to bring the matter to the church and let the more experienced brethren help decide. This is because the new believer may easily either come under excessive accusation of his conscience or he may desist from dealing with anything due to the difficulties involved. What is done in revival meetings can never be compared with what is done in the church. In the former case the new believer has to strike out alone; in the latter case he has the benefit of the fellowship of the church.

LESSON THREE

SELLING ALL

And a certain ruler asked him, saying, Good Teacher,
what shall I do to inherit eternal life? And Jesus said unto
him, Why callest thou me good? none is good, save one,
even God. Thou knowest the commandments, Do not com-
mit adultery, Do not kill, Do not steal, Do not bear false
witness, Honor thy father and mother. And he said, All
these things have I observed from my youth up. And when
Jesus heard it, he said unto him, One thing thou lackest
yet: sell all that thou hast, and distribute unto the poor,
and thou shalt have treasure in heaven: and come, follow
me. But when he heard these things, he became exceeding
sorrowful; for he was very rich. And Jesus seeing him said,
How hardly shall they that have riches enter into the kingdom of God! For it is easier for a camel to enter in through
a needle's eye, than for a rich man to enter into the kingdom of God. And they that heard it said, Then who can be
saved? But he said, The things which are impossible with
men are possible with God. And Peter said, Lo, we have
left our own, and followed thee. And he said unto them,
Verily I say unto you, There is no man that hath left house,
or wife, or brethren, or parents, or children, for the kingdom of God's sake, who shall not receive manifold more in
this time, and in the world to come eternal life.

Luke 18:18–30

And he entered and was passing through Jericho. And behold, a man called by name Zacchaeus; and he was a chief
publican, and he was rich. And he sought to see Jesus who
he was; and could not for the crowd, because he was little
of stature. And he ran on before, and climbed up into a
sycomore tree to see him: for he was to pass that way. And
when Jesus came to the place, he looked up, and said unto
him, Zacchaeus, make haste, and come down; for to-day I
must abide at thy house. And he made haste, and came
down, and received him joyfully. And when they saw it,
they all murmured, saying, He is gone in to lodge with a
man that is a sinner. And Zacchaeus stood, and said unto
the Lord, Behold, Lord, the half of my goods I give to the
poor; and if I have wrongfully exacted aught of any man, I
restore fourfold. And Jesus said unto him, To-day is salvation come to this house, forasmuch as he also is a son of
Abraham. For the Son of man came to seek and to save
that which was lost.

Luke 19:1–10

And all that believed were together, and had all things
common; and they sold their possessions and goods, and
parted them to all, according as any man had need.

Acts 2:44–45

And the multitude of them that believed were of one heart
and soul: and not one of them said that aught of the things
which he possessed was his own; but they had all things
common. And with great power gave the apostles their witness of the resurrection of the Lord Jesus: and great grace
was upon them all. For neither was there among them any
that lacked: for as many as were possessors of lands or
houses sold them, and brought the prices of the things that
were sold, and laid them at the apostles' feet: and distribu-
tion was made unto each, according as any one had need.

Acts 4:32–35

Lay not up for yourselves treasures upon the earth, where moth and rust consume, and where thieves break through and steal: but lay up for yourselves treasures in heaven, where neither moth nor rust doth consume, and where thieves do not break through nor steal: for where thy treasure is, there will thy heart be also. The lamp of the body is the eye: if therefore thine eye be single, thy whole body shall be full of light. But if thine eye be evil, thy whole body shall be full of darkness. If therefore the light that is in thee be darkness, how great is the darkness! No man can serve two masters: for either he will hate the one, and love the other; or else he will hold to one, and despise the other. Ye cannot serve God and mammon.

Matt. 6:19–24

The Prerequisite

To help young believers walk in this path of selling all, the church herself needs to be living in such a state. It would be most difficult for young ones to be told to walk one way and yet to be shown another way. If the church is not a consecrated church, she has no right to speak of consecration. If she is not separated from the world, she is not entitled to mention baptism or separation. If the brethren do not sell all and follow the Lord, what good is it to instruct young believers to sell all? God's children need to live in the way wherewith they wish to help others. This does not rule out the possibility that some of God's specially chosen souls may yet walk in this way even though the church does not take such a position, but it does mean it will be impossible for the most to go along. Should most of the brethren be wholly abandoned to God, it will be easier for newcomers to do likewise. But if we do not give all, how can we expect beginners to lay their all on the altar?

For this path of selling all to be carried through, the local assembly itself must be strong in this respect.

The Lesson of the Young Ruler

Let us start with the example of the young ruler in Luke 18. He was a man of good conduct, not a bad person before God. He had kept all the commandments and had shown due respect to the Lord Jesus by calling Him a good teacher. And the Lord Jesus considered him quite precious, for to meet such a person was rare. Looking upon him, Jesus loved him.

However, the Lord set down one requirement. If anyone desires to serve Him, he must be perfect. Notice what the Lord said: "If thou wouldst be perfect. . . . One thing thou lackest yet" (Matt. 19:21; Lk. 18:22). In other words, the Lord wants those who follow Him to follow Him perfectly, not lacking in anything. People cannot follow God if they have solved ninety and nine of their problems but have yet one problem unsolved. To follow God demands the whole being. It must be all or not at all.

Indeed, this young ruler had kept the commandments from his youth up. He habitually feared God. Yet he lacked one thing. He needed to sell all his property and distribute the proceeds to the poor; then the way would be clear for him to come and follow the Lord.

1. TO FOLLOW THE LORD MEANS TO SELL ALL

Have you seen that no one can possibly follow the Lord if he does not sell all that he has? This exacting demand must be clearly understood. According to the record of the Bible, when the young man heard the saying, he went away sorrowful, for he was one who had great possessions.

Having come so near to the Lord and having seen so clearly too, he yet kept his sorrow even as he determined to keep his wealth. "For the love of money . . . have pierced themselves through with many sorrows" (1 Tim. 6:10). Men may hoard wealth but they cannot hoard happiness. As they accumulate wealth, they also accumulate trouble. In gathering wealth they gather sorrows and problems. Here was a young man who kept his wealth but was unable to follow the Lord. If wealth is what you want, then you need not think of following the Lord. To keep wealth is also to keep your sorrow, for wealth and sorrow always go together.

He who gives up his wealth is a happy man, whereas he who is reluctant to part with it is a sad person. This statement is always true. Those who are greedy of material things dwell in sorrows. May the newly saved Christian seek happiness by laying aside all and following the Lord.

Having watched the young ruler depart sorrowfully, the Lord added a comment: "How hardly shall they that have riches enter into the kingdom of God!" The question at first was: "What shall I do to inherit eternal life?" Now it is related to the matter of entering into the kingdom of God. In connection with this, Peter then asks who can be saved? To be saved, to have eternal life, and to enter into the kingdom of God are all three put together. If you wish to have eternal life, you must forsake all that you have or else you will be hindered. Remember, a rich man (that is, one who trusts in riches) has no way to enter into the kingdom of God. Indeed, the Lord would save such a one if he asked for it. But being saved, he would resign all. This does not mean that he was saved by forsaking his wealth. It simply affirms that once saved he will naturally abandon all.

As it is absolutely impossible for a camel to enter through a needle's eye, so is it equally impossible for a rich man to enter into the kingdom of God. We Christians are all like camels, big or small camels, but nevertheless camels. Thus when Peter heard those words, he was frightened and therefore remonstrated, "Then who can be saved?" Peter after all was a Bible teacher. He combined the statement our Lord said to the young ruler with His latter comment and concluded that the rich cannot enter into the kingdom of God and that only those who have sold all can have eternal life. Peter did not feel easy with this teaching. If eternal life is to be obtained by works and not by faith, if the rich must sell all before he can enter into the kingdom of God, who then can be saved? Who is able to sell first and then obtain eternal life? Who is able to make himself poor before he is saved?

2. THE REAL ISSUE

The Lord Jesus answered with one sentence, and in this one sentence is the crux of the whole problem. Let us too hold onto this word: "The things which are impossible with men are possible with God." It is quite clear that such a thing as abandoning all to enter into the kingdom of God is unheard of in this world. The Lord acknowledges this as humanly impossible. What was wrong with the young ruler was not his inability to sell all, but rather his sorrowful departure. God knows it is impossible for men to sell and distribute all to the poor. But when the young man sadly left, he seemed to conclude that this was also impossible with God. Of course it is wrong for me not to forsake my all, but does not the Lord know all about it? Therefore the Lord declares: what is impossible with men is possible with God. How can anyone get a camel through a needle's eye? Impossible. Similarly, people on this earth all love wealth and to ask them to sell all is to ask for the impossible. But if I go away with sorrow, then I am really wrong, for I have limited the power of God.

The young ruler could not abandon all, but God can do it. In other words, the Lord was prepared to give grace to the young man if he had only cried, "O Lord, I cannot abandon my wealth, but give me grace. What is impossible with me is possible with You. Enable me to do what I am unable to do. Lord, I just am too attached to my wealth to give it up and distribute it to the poor and then come and follow You, but You can make me to be what You want me to be." The mistake he made was to not pray, ask, and believe. He ought not to have sorrowfully departed. Man's failure is not due to his weakness, but to his not accepting God's strength. It is not in his inability but in not allowing God to enable him. He cannot do it, but why not let God deliver him? This is what the Lord stresses here. The things which are impossible with men are possible with God. Our Lord wanted to prove to the young ruler what God can do, but he, instead, went away with the conclusion that the thing was impossible to him.

Let us therefore see that there is always a way for us. If we can gladly forsake all, as Peter did, then we should thank God for that. But if we feel hesitant, as the young ruler did, then there is yet a way open to us. We merely need to bow our heads and say to the Lord, "I cannot," and He will undertake for us.

3. A Christian Must Be Absolute

Peter, after hearing what the Lord said, asked: "Lo, we have left our own, and followed thee," as if to say, "What then will happen to us?" The Lord's answer shows it is

41

well to leave all, for He said: anyone who has left house or wife or brethren or parents or children for My sake and for the sake of the gospel shall receive manifold more in this time, and in the world to come, eternal life. He does desire us to follow Him and to forsake all for His sake and the gospel's sake. This clearly indicates the absolute necessity for a Christian to forsake all and follow the Lord.

Young believers need to know that unless they forsake all they cannot follow the Lord. We have a good example of this in the twelve apostles. When they were called by the Lord, they gladly and promptly left their boats, nets, and all and followed Him. They forsook without hesitancy. How we thank God for new believers like them. Nevertheless, even if some, like the young ruler, feel hesitant to sell all, they still are shown a way to follow the Lord. With men it is impossible, but with God all things are possible.

Let us remember: of the thirteen who were called, eleven followed eagerly, one pretended to follow, and one hesitated. The one who pretended was Judas and the one who hesitated was the young ruler. When the word of the Lord is proclaimed, do not imagine that of those who respond, there will be only one who truly follows the Lord. No, the Bible tells us there was only one who was afraid to follow. If the whole church walks in this way, there need be no fear of having too many young rulers. Such people do exist, but they are only occasionally encountered. Of the thirteen, eleven were quite absolute.

The Lesson of Zacchaeus

Zacchaeus was a Jew, but he worked for the Roman government. From the Jewish standpoint, he was a traitor, because he cooperated with the Roman Empire. He helped the Roman Empire collect taxes from his own people. Furthermore, he was a sinner. He did not have a good character like the young ruler who kept the commandments from his youth. Like other tax collectors, he was greedy and extorted as much as he could. He certainly had earned his poor reputation. Yet, the Lord Jesus passed by. Great is His power to attract people to Him. "No man can come to me, except the Father that sent me draw him" (John 6:44). So this tax collector was drawn by God to His Son. Due to his short stature, Zacchaeus climbed a tree to see Jesus. The Lord looked at him but did not preach a sermon to him. He did not say, "You must repent and confess your sins," nor did He reproach him for extortion and greediness; neither did He require him to sell all, give to the poor, and follow Him. No sermon was preached, just a few simple words were said: "Zacchaeus, make haste, and come down; for to-day I must abide at thy house." Not a single word of exhortation. How strange that the Lord should speak nothing of the truth of regeneration as in John, chapter 3, or of the living water as in chapter 4, or of the light as in chapter 8, or of the grain of wheat as in chapter 12. Neither did He speak on Christian conduct as found in Matthew, chapters 5 to 7. He neither preached nor exhorted. It was just a personal contact, a private encounter. A heart which desired the Lord was met by the Lord who chose him. Zacchaeus knew nothing at all of any doctrine.

The people standing around at that time began to murmur. They thought it highly unfair for Jesus of Nazareth to go to no house but that of such a sinner. They all knew Zacchaeus and what sort of a person he was. As soon as they heard what the Lord said, they felt hurt.

43

Take note of the point of emphasis here. The Lord did not preach any doctrine, but simply said, "I must abide at thy house." That simple word, however, was sufficient. Actually, He had not yet come to Zacchaeus' house; He merely suggested His coming. But this was enough, for wherever the Lord is, there the love of money departs. When He comes, all those problems are solved. His desiring to go to Zacchaeus' house was as powerful as if He were already there. Just that simple statement, "I must abide at thy house," made Zacchaeus bankrupt, for he stood and declared, "Behold, Lord, the half of my goods I give to the poor; and if I have wrongfully exacted aught of any man, I restore fourfold."

The young ruler was exhorted by the Lord, but he failed to obey; Zacchaeus was not even persuaded and yet he fully followed the Lord's wish. Both were rich, and generally speaking, the older a person is the more he loves money. But here it was the older one who let go his money. The young ruler represents "impossible with men," whereas Zacchaeus represents "possible with God." To sell all and follow the Lord is not a small matter. To do so is not easy, for who would be willing to forsake his wealth? Unless he had gone mad, no man would part with all his possessions at once. But the story of Zacchaeus demonstrates to us that what is impossible for man is possible for God. Zacchaeus did what the Lord wished without hearing or accepting any doctrine. This illustrates how easily it can be done.

A Camel Passes Through the Needle's Eye

When God is at work, the camel passes through the needle's eye. In Luke 18 a camel circles around the needle's eye hesitantly and fails to go through, but in chapter

19 that camel swiftly passes through the eye of the needle. Chapter 18 tells us it is impossible with men; chapter 19 shows us all things are possible with God. For the world, selling all is madness, but for those looking to the Lord it can be quickly done.

How could Zacchaeus do this? Because, first, he was a son of Abraham, and second, salvation had come to his house that day. He did it, not because he himself was able to nor because he had cried and prayed and meditated in his heart on all that the Lord had said, and thus had finally with gnashing teeth given in. He did not surrender a bit today and a bit tomorrow until he was forced to surrender all. Neither by determination nor by struggling nor by consideration did he do it. Then how was it that he could dissolve his house in such a way? Had he not hoarded for decades, braved many dangers and fallen into great disrepute in order to build up his house? But now he deliberatcly destroyed it all—because salvation had come to his house. He did not save himself; it was the Lord who saved him.

When salvation comes to a house, the power of the Lord also comes to it. Read together the two places where Zacchaeus' house is mentioned: "To-day I must abide at thy house," and "To-day is salvation come to this house." It is clear that the Lord is the salvation. The coming of the Lord to our house is the coming of salvation to us. When the Lord comes, salvation comes and power comes too.

"For the Son of Man came to seek and to save that which was lost" (Lk. 19:10). This is a famous verse in Christianity. The Son of Man came to do one thing, to seek those who are lost in wealth. All who love money are lost persons. The Lord today is seeking for such lost ones. He found Zacchaeus and He found us too. We were once

45

lost, but now the Lord has found us. Therefore, our problems likewise can be solved. Money will lose its power over us.

God's Way for Today

Take note of these two chapters, Luke 18 and 19: in the one the young ruler was charged by the Lord to sell all, but went away sadly; in the other Zacchaeus abandoned all without even being asked. In His days on this earth our Lord required people to forsake all and follow Him. Likewise the church, shortly after its founding, did the same thing. In Acts 2 and 4 we find that at the beginning of the church all things are held in common; that is, not one of the believers said that any of the things he possessed was his own. In other words, the hand of the Lord was upon all those who were saved. Once they had gained eternal life, their possessions began to lose their grip, and, in quite a natural way, they sold their houses and properties.

Applying this principle to those of us today who come to follow the Lord, it should also be quite natural to us that our many possessions be touched by Him. Our attitude should be turned so that we no longer regard these things as our own. No one then will say that this or that thing belongs to me. No one will claim anything as peculiarly his own. Whatever there is, you may use it just as much as I may. Whatever money there is in my pocket may be put in your pocket as well. Whatever clothes I have, you may wear them too. This is the attitude one must have towards possessions. From my own personal life let me tell you something which may sound like a joke. For nearly twenty years, I have had the habit of purchasing a dozen or half-dozen of anything I buy. Some brothers wonder why I buy so much. For example: I need a pair of sunglasses. So I say to the Lord, "O God, if You really want to give me a pair of sunglasses, then You must give me six pair." Why? Because I feel more peaceful wearing my sunglasses after I have given away five pair to the brethren. Or if I buy a safety razor, I usually buy a dozen; razor blades, a gross. Why do I do this? Because if I buy only one safety razor, it would be exclusively for my own use. Of course, I cannot give a razor to each and everyone of a thousand or two thousand brothers. But it does bring a different flavor if I give to some brothers before I use mine. Otherwise, I would tend to feel that this razor belongs exclusively to me. Those brothers and sisters who have known me over the years will, I think, know this habit of mine. Usually I purchase in dozens, though I only use one. Thus shall we be delivered from things.

The Principle of "All Things in Common"

Let us not hold on to things too tightly. This garment of mine—maybe the Lord does not want me to have it permanently; maybe it should be given away tomorrow. Therefore it is better that I make two or three garments instead of one. This is the flavor that we hould maintain. Everytime we buy things, we should not think only of ourselves but of others as well. This is not to say that we should not buy anything new; it simply suggests that there must always be the savor of having all things in common. Of course I am not talking about any particular thing or action; I only stress the particular principle. We should never think of ourselves only but should always maintain the principle of holding all things in common.

What, then, is the lesson God would have us learn? First of all, let us learn not to be rooted in this world, but to hold all things loosely. To be so delivered from the things of the world is not a small matter. How stingy are the people of this world! How many are the miserly people! They are close-fisted not only in big things but in small things as well. They actually pennypinch in everything.

The more we read the second and fourth chapters of Acts, the more we are convinced that we should not hold on to anything, but should rather hold all things in common. God's children must be liberal towards others of God's children. Whether or not we actually sell our property and give to the poor, the sentiment is the same. We must be willing to share with others. Let us not hold onto anything, even to such a small article as a knife or a pen. We need to let all things go. If we obey in this, God will not suffer us to have less; yea, He will even give us more.

So, this is the example of the early church. In the beginning, the twelve disciples said to the Lord, "We have left our own, and followed thee." During Pentecost, at the first revival, the three thousand and the five thousand quite naturally did the same thing. First, it was the twelve who forsook all and followed the Lord without hearing any teaching on it. The Lord did not tell them to sell all; He merely said, "Come ye after me" (Matt. 4:19). They responded to the call by abandoning all. In like manner, the apostles did not instruct the three thousand or the five thousand to sell their possessions; those believers just did it spontaneously. This is what the church has been practicing throughout the centuries. And this is what we too must do today. It would be tragic if such a practice were not continued.

God or Mammon

Let us return to Matthew 6 where it says we can only serve one master. We cannot serve God and mammon. Mammon (or riches) is an idol which many have served over the past years. Such service gets a firm grip on the heart. Now, though, if we are going to serve God, we must choose whom to serve—God or mammon. We cannot serve both. What does the Lord say? "For where thy treasure is, there will thy heart be also" (Matt. 6:21). Once a brother told me: "My treasure is on earth but my heart is in heaven." Such a brother should be exhibited in a Christian museum as a rarity! The Lord says it cannot be, but he invents a can be. Is it not greater than a miracle? However, the word of the Lord is candid and sure. One's heart always follows the treasure. There is no escape from it. No matter how one reasons, his heart goes after his treasure.

"Lay not up for yourselves treasures upon the earth" (Matt. 6:19). If you do, you will end up serving mammon and not God. You cannot serve both God and mammon. You must choose either one or the other. How detrimental it would be to choose mammon, for such treasure is subject to moth and rust and thieves. Let us, therefore, learn to serve God. Let us give all that we have to God and maintain the simplest kind of life here on this earth.

CONSECRATION

And for Aaron's sons thou shalt make coats, and thou shalt make for them girdles, and head-tires shalt thou make for them, for glory and beauty. And thou shalt put them upon Aaron thy brother, and upon his sons with him, and shalt anoint them, and consecrate them, and sanctify them, that they may minister unto me in the priest's office. And thou shalt make them linen breeches to cover the flesh of their nakedness; from the loins even unto the thighs they shall reach: and they shall be upon Aaron, and upon his sons, when they go in unto the tent of meeting, or when they come near unto the altar to minister in the holy place; that they bear not iniquity, and die: it shall be a statute for ever unto him and unto his seed after him.

Ex. 28:40–43

And he presented the ram of the burnt-offering: and Aaron and his sons laid their hands upon the head of the ram. And he killed it; and Moses sprinkled the blood upon the altar round about. And he cut the ram into its pieces; and Moses burnt the head, and the pieces, and the fat. And he washed the inwards and the legs with water; and Moses burnt the whole ram upon the altar: it was a burnt-offering for a sweet savor: it was an offering made by fire unto Jehovah; as Jehovah commanded Moses. And he presented the other ram, the ram of consecration: and Aaron and his sons laid their hands upon the head of the ram. And he slew it; and Moses took of the blood thereof, and put it upon the tip of Aaron's right ear, and upon the thumb of his right hand, and upon the great toe of his right foot. And he brought Aaron's sons; and Moses put of the blood upon the tip of their right ear, and upon the thumb of their right hand, and upon the great toe of their right foot: and Moses sprinkled the blood upon the altar round about. And he took the fat, and the fat tail, and all the fat that was upon the inwards, and the caul of the liver, and the two kidneys, and their fat, and the right thigh: and out of the basket of unleavened bread, that was before Jehovah, he took one unleavened cake, and one cake of oiled bread, and one wafer, and placed them on the fat, and upon the right thigh: and he put the whole upon the hands of Aaron, and upon the hands of his sons, and waved them for a wave-offering before Jehovah. And Moses took them from off their hands, and burnt them on the altar upon the burnt-offering: they were a consecration for a sweet savor: it was an offering made by fire unto Jehovah.

Lev. 8:18–28

Neither present your members unto sin as instruments of unrighteousness; but present yourselves unto God, as alive from the dead, and your members as instruments of right-eousness unto God. Know ye not, that to whom ye present yourselves as servants unto obedience, his servants ye are whom ye obey; whether of sin unto death, or of obedience unto righteousness? I speak after the manner of men be-cause of the infirmity of your flesh: for as ye presented your members as servants to uncleanness and to iniquity unto iniquity, even so now present your members as servants to righteousness unto sanctification.

Rom. 6:13,16,19

I beseech you therefore, brethren, by the mercies of God, to present your bodies a living sacrifice, holy, acceptable to

God, which i... ...ned
according to ... ...e re-
newing of yo... ...good
and acceptab... ...ough
the grace tha... ...mong
you, not to t... ...ght to
think; but so... ...s God
hath dealt to

12:1–3

Or know ye ... ...ie Holy
Spirit which ... ...id ye are
not your ow ... ...rify God
therefore in

. 6:19–20

For the lov... ...e we thus
judge, that ... ...nd he died
for all, that ... ...unto themselves, but ... ...d and rose
again.

II Cor. 5:14–15

In order to build up a new believer, the first problem to solve is the matter of consecration. But whether or not he can take in this lesson depends largely on how well he has been saved. If the gospel has not been well presented, the one who comes to the Lord Jesus may consider himself as doing God a great favor. For a person like him to be a Christian adds much glory to Christianity! Under such an illusion how can any one speak to him about consecration? Even a queen has to be brought to the place where she gladly lays her crown at the Lord's feet. We need to all realize that it is we who are favored by the Lord in being loved and saved. Only then can we willingly lay down everything.

However, consecration is one of the most difficult doctrines in the Bible. The doctrines of sanctification, of righteousness, and of justification are all clearly defined in the Word of God; but the teaching of consecration seems to be vaguely taught. Almost two thousand years have passed and the subject of consecration has yet to be mastered.

The Word of God seldom touches directly on the subject of consecration. In the New Testament we have Romans 6 and 12; in the Old Testament, Exodus 28 and 29 and Leviticus 8. The New Testament refers to presenting our bodies and the members of our body to God, while the Old Testament deals exclusively with the setting apart for holy service of Aaron and his family. These are the only passages in the entire Bible where consecration is directly mentioned. We do not know why the Word of God touches so little on this first Christian experience of service. But we do know that it is therefore imperative that we understand clearly what little the Bible does directly teach.

The Bases of Consecration

Let us search the New Testament first. There we find how the children of God are constrained by love to live unto the Lord who died and rose again for them (2 Cor. 5:14). The word "constrained" means to be tightly held or to be surrounded so that one cannot escape. When a person is moved by love, he will experience such a sensation. Love will bind him and thus he is helpless.

Love, therefore, is the basis of consecration. No one can consecrate himself without sensing the love of the Lord. He has to see the Lord's love before he can ever consecrate his life. It is futile to talk about consecration if the love of the

Lord is not seen. Having seen the Lord's love, consecration will be the inevitable consequence.

However, consecration is also based on right or divine prerogative. This is the truth we find in I Corinthians 6:19-20. "Or know ye not that your body is a temple of the Holy Spirit which is in you, which ye have from God? and ye are not your own; for you have been bought with a price: glorify God therefore in your body." Today among Christians this matter of being bought with a price may not be clearly understood. But to the Corinthians at the time of the Roman Empire, it was perfectly clear. Why? Because at that time they had human markets. Just as one could go to the market to buy chicken or duck, so one could buy human beings in the human market. The only difference was that whereas food prices were more or less established, in the human market the price of each soul was established by bidding at auction. Whoever bid the highest price got the man, and whoever owned the slave had absolute power over him. Paul uses this metaphor to show us what our Lord has done for us and how He gave His life as the ransom to purchase us back to God. The Lord paid a great price—even His own life. And today, because of this work of redemption, we give up our rights and forfeit our sovereignty. We are no longer our own, for we belong to the Lord; therefore we must glorify God in our bodies. We are bought with a price, even the blood of the cross. Since we are bought, we become His by right, by divine prerogative.

On the one hand, for the sake of love we choose to serve Him; and on the other hand, by right we are not our own. we must follow Him; we cannot do otherwise. According to the right of redemption, we are His; and according to the love which redemption generates in us, we must live for Him. One basis for consecration is legal right and the other basis is responsive love. Consecration is thus based on the love which surpasses human feeling as well as on right according to law. For these two reasons, we cannot but belong to the Lord.

Young believers should thoroughly understand this. You are bought back by the Lord. You are like a slave whom the Lord purchased with the highest bid. Hence for you to be a free person is totally out of the question. Christ, the Son of God has bought you not with silver and gold, but with His precious blood. Herein is love; such love ought to constrain all the young ones not to live for themselves from this day forward.

The Real Meaning of Consecration

We should know that being constrained by love is not yet consecration; nor is seeing the Lord's right yet true consecration. After one has been constrained by love and has seen the Lord's prerogative, he needs to do something additional. This extra step puts him in the position of consecration. Being constrained by the Lord's love and knowing that he has been purchased, he quietly sets himself apart from everything in order to be wholly the Lord's. This is the consecration depicted in the Old Testament. It is the acceptance of a holy office, the office of serving the Lord. "O Lord, being loved, what else can I do than to separate myself from everything that I may serve You? Hereafter no one may use my hands or feet or mouth or ears, for these my two hands are to do Your works, my two feet to walk in Your way, my mouth to sing Your praise, and my ears to listen to Your voice." This is consecration.

Suppose you purchase a slave and bring him home. At the door of your house, the man kneels and does you homage, saying, "Master, you have bought me. Today I gladly hearken to your words." For you to have purchased him is one thing, but his kneeling before you and proclaiming his desire to serve you is something else. Because you have purchased him, he acknowledges your right. But because you have loved him even though he is such a man, he proclaims himself wholly yours. This alone is consecration. Consecration is more than love, more than purchasing; *it is the action which follows love and purchasing.* Henceforth the one who consecrates himself is separated from everything in this world, from all his former masters. Hereafter he will do nothing but what his Master commands. He restricts himself to doing only the things of that one Master. This is what consecration really means.

They Who Are Consecrated

Let us now turn to Exodus 28 and 29 with Leviticus 8:18–28. When we read these passages, we are immediately touched by the fact that consecration is something very special. There are so many people in this world, yet no one is able to consecrate himself to the Lord. The entire nation of Israel was chosen by God, but not the entire nation became a consecrated nation. Not all the twelve tribes of Israel were able to enter into consecration, for only the tribe of Levi was chosen. And not even the whole tribe of Levi was consecrated; one family alone, the family of Aaron was consecrated.

This indicates that consecration is not a matter for the world, for the chosen people, for the twelve tribes, or for the Levites; it belongs exclusively to one family. One has to be of that family before he may be consecrated. If he does not belong to that particular family, he has no way to consecrate himself. Only those of this one family, the house of Aaron, may become priests.

Thank God, today we belong to this family, for all who believe in the Lord are of this household (see Revelation 1:5–6). Today *all* the redeemed ones are priests, chosen by God to be priests. Formerly, only those of the house of Aaron were consecrated; anyone else who dared to intrude was immediately cut off. Today, too, remember that only those chosen by God can be consecrated; only people of the one family may be consecrated. But, thank God, today we do belong to this family, for God has chosen us to be priests.

One thing is clear: men do not choose to consecrate themselves to God; it is God who chooses men to be consecrated to Him. All who consider themselves as doing a favor for God by forsaking all to serve Him are actually strangers to consecration. Let them beat a hasty retreat, for they are not the chosen. No one who thinks of service as rendering God a favor and an honor is a chosen one. Who can set himself apart to do the Lord's work? It is God who favors us to have a part in His exclusive work. It is God who gives glory and beauty to us. The Old Testament priest wore two garments, one for glory and one for beauty. In consecration, God clothes us with glory and with beauty. It is God who selects us to serve Him. Let us boastingly declare what a Lord we have. This is what consecration is.

May we realize that consecration means we are chosen for the honor of serving God. Consecration is God granting us glory. We should kneel and pray: "Thank God that I may have a part in His service. Yes, there are many things in the world, but in this one thing I am really privileged to participate." In consecration, we are being exalted; we are not making a sacrifice. Indeed, we do sacrifice, but there is not the consciousness of making any sacrifice. Consecration demands the highest sacrifice, yet it is filled with the sense of glory and not with the awareness of sacrifice.

The Way of Consecration

Take a closer look at Leviticus 8. There are four things to be offered: a bullock of sin-offering; two rams, one of burnt-offering, the other of consecration; and a basket of unleavened bread for a wave-offering.

This is a clear picture of the way of consecration. The first problem which faces one who is to be consecrated to God is atonement. The matter of atonement is a big one, so it requires a big animal, a bullock to solve it. Whoever is to be consecrated must be saved, must belong to the Lord. This, being the foundation of consecration, is a tremendous work and therefore requires a big sacrifice like a bullock to accomplish it.

What follows are the two rams: one as a burnt-offering to be burnt, the other as a consecration-offering to enable Aaron to serve God hereafter. A burnt-offering has to be wholly burnt. The priests are not allowed to eat of its flesh since every part of it must be burnt. Hence it is a step further than the sin-offering. The sin-offering merely solves the problem of our sins, but the burnt-offering gives us acceptance before God. The Lord Jesus bore our sins on the cross; this is the atoning work of our Lord. He rent the veil of the temple in His death, rent it from top to bottom so that He might bring us to the Holiest of all; this is the burnt-offering. Both offerings start at the same place, both beginning with sinners. But sin-offering only atones our sins, while burnt-offering brings sinners to God for acceptance. So burnt-offering makes us accepted in the beloved Son. It goes further than sin-offering, for it speaks of the fragrance of the Lord Jesus in God's presence and hence His acceptance by the Father. Today by offering up a burnt-offering, we too are accepted. Thus we have negatively the forgiveness of sin through the sin-offering, and positively our acceptance in the Lord Jesus.

After the slaying of the first ram, the second ram was slain. The blood of the second ram was put upon the tip of the right ear of Aaron and his sons, and upon the thumb of their right hand, and upon the great toe of their right foot. This was called the offering of consecration and was not completely burnt as the burnt-offering ram was. This ram's blood was first put on the tip of the right ear, the thumb of the right hand, and the great toe of the right foot of the person consecrated. This means that according to the acceptance which Christ has before God, I now stand in the position of a servant who hearkens to God's voice, does His will, and walks in His path. Hereafter my ears, my hands, and my feet belong exclusively to God. Since I have been accepted in Christ, I present my whole being to the Lord.

Where the mark of blood is, there is the ground of God's prerogative. Where the sign of blood is, there is the call of love. The blood both testifies that I am purchased by the Lord and bears witness that He has loved me. The blood here is the price which Christ paid for my redemption and it is also the love of which the New Testament speaks. The ram has been slain, so I offer up my whole being. Thus I become a living sacrifice, for blood is upon me. Though I am alive, yet have I been wholly consecrated. I have presented myself as a living sacrifice to God.

Note especially the wave-offering which follows the killing of the second ram. The putting of blood on the tip of the right ear, the thumb of the right hand, and the great toe of the right foot of the one to be consecrated is still a preparation for consecration. Consecration comes when Moses

> took the fat, and the fat tail, and all the fat that was upon the inwards, and the caul of the liver, and the two kidneys, and their fat, and the right thigh (or shoulder): and out of the basket of unleavened bread, that was before Jehovah, he took one unleavened cake, and one cake of oiled bread, and one wafer, and placed them on the fat, and upon the right thigh: and he put the whole upon the hands of Aaron, and upon the hands of his sons, and waved them for a wave-offering before Jehovah. And Moses took them from off their hands, and burnt them on the altar upon the burnt-offering: they were a consecration for a sweet savor: it was an offering made by fire unto Jehovah.
>
> Lev. 8:25–28

All who study typology agree that the shoulder and the bread represent two different aspects of the Lord Jesus. Shoulder is where strength is. The shoulder of the ram shows us the divine character of the Lord Jesus just as the fat points to the glory of God. Bread reveals His humanity. He is an unleavened, spotless, perfect man. He is full of the Holy Spirit, most sensitive and most tender. His inward feeling and spiritual sense are exceedingly fine. He is not rude but gentle, like a thin cake or wafer which can be broken by a mere touch. These were put in Aaron's hands to be waved before God. First Aaron's hands were filled and then the things from his hands were burnt on the burnt-offering. This is called consecration.

Let us add here a little explanation. In Hebrew the word, "consecration," actually means, "to fill the hands." The hands were at first empty, but then they are filled. At the time that Aaron's hands were filled, that was the time of his consecration. His hands were so full that he could not hold anything else; this is consecration. In his hands he held the shoulder and fat of the ram and the unleavened bread; this too is consecration. To be fully occupied with the divinity as well as the humanity of the Lord, with the divine strength and the unleavened life of the Lord, with the Holy Spirit and with the Lord's sensitivity—this is the time of consecration.

God called Aaron and his family to serve Him as priests. But Aaron could not come imprudently. He must have his sins solved and he himself must be accepted in Christ. His hands must do God's bidding, his feet must walk God's way, and his ears must hear God's word. Further, his hands, being the highest expression of service, needed to be filled with Christ. Only then was he consecrated. What then is consecration? It is simply doing what Paul urged: "I beseech you therefore, brethren, by the mercies of God, to present your bodies a living sacrifice, holy, acceptable to God, which is your spiritual service." We need to come to the Lord and see that there is only one way for us to spend our life, and that is, to serve God. We have no other way but that of serving God.

In order to serve God, I present my whole body. Hereafter no one can borrow my ears to listen to another's voice, or my hands to do another's bidding, or my feet to walk another's path. Aside from the Lord, no one can use me any more. I am here for the service of God. My whole body is devoted to His service. I have handed myself over like a sacrifice; I am wholly devoted to Him. I even take a further step: I have my two hands filled with Christ (here the ears, hands and feet are joined in one); I wave and I heave what are in my hands. This action is called consecration.

Therefore consecration means that having been touched by the Lord's love and having seen the Lord's right, I come to God and beg to serve Him. I come on my own accord, not because I am called. I pray: "O God, I now belong to the Lord, for I am bought by Him. Formerly I was under the table hoping to eat of the crumbs that fell down, but hereafter, O God, do not let me serve You under the table. Once I received grace like a dog, but now I cannot serve You at the door as a dog. I today choose to serve You. I know I am accepted in Christ. May I not be permitted to have a little part in Your service? I ask for Your mercy that I may be allowed to serve You. You did not pass over me but You saved me. Now I request of You once again, do not pass me by but let me be among the many who serve You."

Thus we come to the Lord and are accepted. Thus have we laid everything before Him to be for His use. Romans 12 tells us our whole bodies must be presented; this coincides with the ears, hands and feet of the Old Testament. So now the Old and the New Testament join in one.

The Aim of Consecration

Consecration aims not at preaching or working for God, but in serving God. The word "service" in the original bears the sense of "waiting on," that is, waiting on God in order to serve Him. Consecration does not necessarily involve incessant labor, for its aim is to wait upon God. If He wishes us to stand, we stand; if He wants us to wait, we wait; and if He desires us to run, we run. This is the true meaning of "waiting on" Him.

What God requires of us is to present our bodies to Him, not for the purpose of ascending the pulpit or of evangelizing far distant lands, but of waiting upon Him. Some may indeed have to accept the pulpit, because they are sent there by God. Some may be constrained to go to distant lands, for they are commissioned by God to go. The work itself varies but the time consumed remains the same—our lifetime. We need to learn to wait on God. We offer our bodies that we may be those who serve.

Once we become Christians, we must serve God for life. As soon as a medical doctor becomes a Christian, medicine recedes from being his vocation to being his avocation. So will it be for the engineer. The Lord's demand occupies the first priority; serving God becomes the major job. Should the Lord permit, I can do some medical or engineering work to maintain a living, but I will not be able to make either of them my life work. Some of the early disciples were fishermen, but after they followed the Lord they did not hope any more to be great and successful fishermen. They might be allowed to fish occasionally, but their destiny was altered.

May God be gracious to us, especially to young believers, that we may all see how our vocation has been changed. Let all the professors, doctors, nurses, engineers, and industrialists see that their vocation is now to serve God. Their past vocations have receded to avocations. They should not be too ambitious in their special fields, though the Lord may still give some of them special positions We who serve God cannot expect to be prosperous in the world, for these two are contradictory. Hereafter we are to serve God alone; we have no other way or destiny.

In consecration, our prayer is: "O Lord, You have given me the opportunity and privilege to come before You and serve You. Lord, I am Yours. Henceforth my ears, hands, and feet, being bought by the blood, are exclusively Yours. The world can no longer use them, nor will I use them either." What, then, is the result? The result will be holiness, for the fruit of consecration is holiness. In Exodus 28 we have consecration on the one hand and holiness to the Lord on the other.

We need to be brought to see that after we become Christians, we are spoiled for everything else. This does not mean we will be less faithful in our secular jobs. No, we must be subject to authorities and faithfully fulfill our tasks. But we have seen before God that our life must be spent in the way of serving God; all other jobs are side lines.

The Song of Consecration

There is a chorus which runs: "I am His, I am His. Glory to His name, For I am His." Though the refrain is simple, yet it must have been written by one who knew what consecration is. Such a song can only be sung by redeemed ones. And only redeemed ones can consecrate themselves.

I feel strongly during these years that the way consecration is preached is wrong. It should not be preached as if we were begging people to consecrate; we should tell people instead that the way is now open for consecration. If I hang out a placard, announcing that I am commissioned to find those with ability to work for the president, I suppose many will invite me for dinner; many will seek for the job of serving the president. Is it not strange that we beg people to come to serve God? Let me tell you: there is a way open for you to serve the Lord of Hosts. You come to serve God, not to do God a favor.

Perhaps, though, I desire to serve God but am uncertain as to whether I will be accepted. However, the Old Testament passages show us that we do have God's permission to consecrate ourselves. The New Testament confirms this by saying that by the compassions of God I should present myself to Him, for it is my spiritual service. To be privileged to be God's slaves is our greatest honor.

STUDYING THE BIBLE

The Importance of Studying the Bible

No good Christian should be ignorant of the Word of God, for God's way of speaking to men today is to reiterate the words He has already spoken. It is extremely rare to find God speaking to anyone with words that are not found in the Bible. Although at times God does speak directly to some who have gone on far with the Lord, yet even these utterances are largely words which He has already set forth in the Scriptures. God's speaking, then, is His repeating what He has said before. Young believers, if unfamiliar with what God has already spoken, create a problem for God in that they do not have the foundation for God to speak to them.

The Bible is the Word of God. It reveals to us all that God has done for us in the past. It also shows us in what ways God has led men to know Him in days gone by. In order to know the richness and fullness of God's provision for us, we must study the Bible. And to understand by what steps God will lead us to Himself, we also need to study the Bible.

Furthermore, when God desires to use us to speak for Him, He u ually uses the words He already has spoken. Should we be ignorant of these words, it is difficult for God to speak through us. We then will be useless persons before Him. Thus we need to store the Word of Christ richly in our hearts that we may hear those words which God wants to speak to us now and also that we may know how God has walked in the past.

The Bible is a big book and a serious one. If we were to spend the whole of our life in the study of it, we would but touch its fringes. How can any believer know the Word without spending time on it? It is absolutely impossible. Thus young people especially ought to be diligent in studying God's Word so that as they reach middle age and then old age, they will have a rich supply of the Word for the needs both of themselves and of others.

Whosoever wishes to know God must study God's Word well. Every new believer needs to recognize the importance of studying God's Word at the very start of his Christian life. Let me be very frank with you: there are too few who really know the Bible. This generation is far inferior in the study of the Word. We do not see many of those giants of the Word of four or five decades ago. Today we mostly meet superficial readers. Where can we find people who have thoroughly studied the Bible? This generation is way behind in understanding of the Word. We are not talking here about spiritual life but rather about understanding. People may be able to get something of a devotional nature out of the Book, but few today really study the Bible.

The hope now is in the young people. We expect to have within these five or ten years a number of people who have really studied the Bible. This is not as simple as it sounds, for it requires lots of time. There must be a solid founda-tion in God's Word; otherwise nothing can be built. The expounding of the Bible that we hear today is wholly inadequate. Such a shallow life in the church is a disgrace before God.

How to Study the Bible

How, then, should we study the Bible? Four basic principles are:

(a) Find or discover facts
(b) Memorize the Word
(c) Analyze, deduce and compare the Word
(d) Receive enlightenment from God

However varied may be the external methods, the basic principles of studying the Word remain unchanged. And the order given above should also be kept: first fact finding, next memorizing, then analyzing, and finally receiving enlightenment.

The Bible contains many spiritual facts which to the spiritually blind are hidden. If one discovers any fact in the Bible, he already has half the light and hence has fulfilled half of the study purpose. It is therefore absolutely necessary to find facts; otherwise we will not be able to receive God's enlightenment, for the light of God shines only on the facts in His Word. Why does God speak in this way or in that way? Through analysis, comparison, and deduction we are open to enlightenment. Thus shall we be fed and thus shall we be able to feed others. If we study the Bible carelessly, God's Word will leak away and we will not know what is in it.

For example: the earth's gravitational force is a fact. It is a universal law, yet it awaited Newton to discover this law of gravitation. Before the time of Newton, though for thousands of years the force of gravitation had been there, yet the law had remained undiscovered. One day Newton was resting underneath an apple tree and an apple fell on his head. Through this incident he discovered the law of gravitation. The question was not whether there was or was not such a fact; the question was simply the discovery of the fact.

It is likewise a matter of great importance to be able to discover cardinal facts in the Bible. For example, what the Bible says and what it does not say are deeply significant. Why does it say things differently in different places? God has forbidden that a single word of the original Bible be changed. Why then in some instances is the singular number used whereas in other instances it is the plural? Why sometimes are years clearly mentioned and other times many years just skipped over? All these are facts to be noticed.

For the above reasons, one who studies the Bible must be a careful person before God. He cannot afford to be inattentive. He must be a single-minded individual, for the Word of God is pure. As soon as he hears God's Word, he should know where the emphasis lies. But many Christians read the Word without hearing anything. They find neither its facts nor its keys.

1. SAMPLES OF COMPARATIVE METHOD

Let us take some simple illustrations:

"IN CHRIST"

In studying God's Word, we will see that the New Testament only uses terms such as "in the Lord," "in Christ," "in Christ Jesus," never does it say "in Jesus" or "in Jesus

70

Christ." This is what we call the discovery of fact. We should try to remember all instances where these terms are employed. Then we should compare them with the terms that are not used. Why in a certain place is the phrase "in Christ" used but not "in Jesus"? Why does it say "in Christ Jesus" but not "in Jesus Christ"? Why does the Bible never once use the term "in Jesus Christ"? As we analyze and compare the Word, we can expect God to give us light that we may see.

We now are shown that "Jesus" is the earthly name of our Lord. "Jesus Christ" means this Jesus will one day be Christ. "Christ" is the name given to Him after His resurrection and anointing by God. "Let all the house of Israel therefore know assuredly, that God has made Him both Lord and Christ, this Jesus whom ye crucified" (Acts 2:36). Hence it is His name of resurrection. Then in Romans we find "Christ Jesus," which means the Christ of today is the Jesus of yesterday. Christ Jesus has become His name now. The term "Jesus Christ" is quite different from that of "Christ Jesus." Christ is formerly Jesus, and Jesus later will be Christ. We can only be in Christ but never in Jesus. We can be in the Lord or in Christ Jesus, but not in Jesus Christ.

When our Lord lived on earth, we could not be in Him. For if we were, we would share His cross and the work of redemption. No, He alone is God's only begotten Son; we have no part in it. His birth in Bethlehem is something we cannot share. Then why is it we can be in Christ? "But of Him are ye in Christ Jesus" (1 Cor. 1:30). It does not say in Jesus, but in Christ Jesus. For we are actively united with Him in His resurrection after He died and was raised from among the dead. There God has made Him Christ; and there by His Spirit God has joined us to Him.

71

"BLOOD" AND "CROSS" IN ROMANS

We know that Romans, chapters 1–8, deal with the redemptive work of the Lord. These eight chapters are further divided into two parts: chapters 1–5:11 form one part and chapters 5:12 through chapter 8 another part. All who study the Bible are amazed by the fact that in the first part the cross is not mentioned whereas in the second part the blood is never referred to. The first part speaks only of the blood but not of the cross; the second part focuses on the cross and not on the blood.

After knowing and memorizing what it is God has spoken and what it is He has not spoken, we can then start to analyze. Basically there are two methods of analysis: one is to dissect in order to scrutinize more carefully; the other is to gather together in order to have a more comprehensive picture. As we individually consider Romans 1–8, maybe within an hour or half an hour we will be given light to see that the forgiveness of sins and justification are by the blood but that deliverance from the power of sin must be through the cross. Deliverance comes not from the blood but from the cross, while forgiveness comes not from the cross but from the blood.

Having memorized sufficient Bible verses, one may attempt to analyze them before God. He may not be able to understand them at first, but after trying for a month or even half a year he may be given understanding. I have mentioned before that if anyone is able to find facts, he has already received half of the light. If one is unable to discover facts, it only proves he has an eye ailment. Young people, therefore should start out as careful readers. He is a careless person who does not seek for facts. He will not know either what God has said or what God has not said. How can this be called the study of the Word of God?

Do remember one thing: whether or not one is able to be a minister of God's Word depends on whether he can find facts while studying the Bible. Each and every minister of God's Word needs to be a vigilant, accurate person. Facts are like mountain peaks, protruding out conspicuously. Only the lazy, the careless, the confused and the insensitive do not know how to read the Bible because they are unable to find the facts of God.

2. SAMPLE OF THE ANALYTICAL METHOD

Let us now turn from the comparative method to the analytical method. For an example, let us use John's record concerning the sending of the Holy Spirit. In reading chapters 14 and 16, we find the promise of the Lord Jesus. Is there anything special in this promise? Consider chapter 14:16–20,

> And I will pray the Father, and he shall give you another Comforter, that he may be with you for ever, even the Spirit of truth: whom the world cannot receive, for it beholdeth him not, neither knoweth him: ye know him; for he abideth with you, and shall be in you. I will not leave you desolate: I come unto you. Yet a little while, and the world beholdeth me no more; but ye behold me: because I live, ye shall live also. In that day ye shall know that I am in my Father, and ye in me, and I in you.

What fact do we here discover? In the first part of this passage, we find the word "he" or "him" is used, but in the second part the pronoun is changed to "I" or "me." There is a shift from "him" to "me."

Having noticed that fact and memorized all these verses, we should now proceed to analyze them. The Lord mentions another Comforter. "Another" implies that this is a second one. For instance, "I will give you another cup," simply means, "I will give you a second cup." "I will ask another one to help you," invariably refers to a second helper. The Father will send you another Comforter, that is, the second Comforter. Since there will be the second Comforter, there must previously have been the first Comforter, just as another helper implies the presence of the first helper, and another cup a first one.

The fact has thus been established that there are two Comforters. What does the Lord say about the second Comforter? "He may be with you for ever." Who is He? We do not seem to know Him, and yet the Lord says, "Whom the world cannot receive; for it beholdeth him not, neither knoweth him: ye know him." Why? "For he abideth with you." Had I been one of the twelve disciples on that day, I would certainly ask: "O Lord! You say the Comforter abides with me, but I neither see Him when I am asleep nor when I am awake. I do not see Him when eating or when walking. In fact, I have never known Him. How can you say that I know Him?"

But notice: immediately following the word, "For he abideth with you and shall be in you," he continues with, "I will not leave you desolate: I come unto you." In analysis, we discover the "he" has changed to "I." In other words, "I" am "he." While the Lord Jesus is on the earth, He is the Comforter; that is, the Holy Spirit in Him is the Comforter. This is seeing light. On earth, the Lord and the Holy Spirit are one, for the latter abides in Him. He is seen and known by the disciples, because He abides with them.

But now, another Comforter is given. The Lord is to die, to be resurrected and to come again. How will He come? He will come in the Holy Spirit so that He may not leave

74

His disciples desolate. "Yet a little while, and the world beholdeth me no more; but ye behold me: because I live, ye shall live also." For a little while you do not see Me, yet after a while you shall see Me again and I will live in you. In verse 17, "he shall be in you," but now in verse 20, "I in you." The "he" above is therefore the "I" of the following verses. The first time it is the Holy Spirit in Christ, the latter time it is Christ in the Holy Spirit. Who is the Holy Spirit? The Holy Spirit is the second self of the Lord Jesus As the Son is the Father's second self, so the Holy Spirit is the second self of the Son. The form alone is changed.

It is therefore evident that the basic principle in studying the Bible is to find facts. It really does not depend on how many chapters one has read or how much he has memorized. If he cannot find facts, he will receive no light from God. For a worker, the ability to find facts in the Bible is a foundational requirement. Paul was one who had great ability in finding facts. Listen to what he says in the third chapter of Galatians. When he read Genesis, he found in God's promise to Abraham, "in thy seed shall all the nations of the earth be blessed" (Gen. 22:18), that seed there is singular, not plural, and therefore points to Christ. Paul had discovered a fact in the Bible. Now there are tens of thousands of facts like the one just mentioned. Whether or not one is rich in God's Word depends largely on his ability to find out facts.

3. SAMPLE OF THE DEDUCTIVE METHOD

Let us turn to illustrate the deductive method: take for instance the matter of making images. Exodus 20:4 commands: "Thou shalt not make unto thee a graven image, nor any likeness of any thing that is in heaven above, or that is in the earth beneath, or that is in the water under the earth." But in Genesis, God Himself says, "Let us make man in our image, after our likeness. . . . And God created man in his own image" (Gen. 1:26–27). Also in Exodus 26, God ordered the people of Israel to "make a veil of blue, and purple, and scarlet, and fine twined linen: with cherubim the work of the skilful workman shall it be made" (v. 31). The cherubim have the likeness of a man; and every one has four faces—that of a man, a lion, an ox and an eagle (Ez. 1:5, 10). This veil is to separate the Holiest from the Holy Place.

After gathering together these passages, the question will naturally be asked: did God contradict Himself? On the one hand He commanded not to make any image and He judged Israel because they made the image of the golden calf; on the other hand He Himself ordered them to make the image of the cherubim. Why does the Bible both permit and forbid the making of images? Why is no image permitted except that of cherubim? To what does the image of the cherubim point? This will lead us to Hebrews. Hebrews 10:20 indicates that the veil typifies the flesh of Christ, meaning the Lord Jesus Himself. In other words, all images are idols except the One who is the image of God. Notice what Genesis 1:26–27 said. When the Godhead was in council, it was decided to make "a man in our image." But when it came to actual creative work, "God created man in *his* own image." In verse 26 it is the plural "our," while in verse 27 it becomes the singular "his." Such transfer from the plural pronoun to the singular is a fact to be reckoned with. It reveals that in the Godhead only one Person has an image, and that Person is Christ. By combining all these passages, we conclude that God rejects all images except the one image—His own Son.

Some Notable Students of the Bible*

Through the centuries many children of God have spent time on the Word of God. Some of the best brains of these two thousand years have been engaged in God's Word. Indeed, God has chosen first rank minds from this world for His Word. This is part of the heritage of the Church.

First, let us mention the lower critics, those who scrutinize the letter of the Bible. People such as Tregelles, Dean Alford, Wordsworth and Westcott are giants among thousands of such critics. Why was such a task necessary? Because there was no printing press when the Bible was first written, and it was a forbidden book too. If anyone was found with a Bible, he could be thrown to the wild beasts. In order to read the Bible, he had to copy it himself. He could only copy a little at a time and he had to copy in a great hurry lest he be found by the police. Under such circumstances, error in copying was inevitable. Even with today's typesetting, mistakes are unavoidable; how much more was the possibility of making mistakes when every word had to be copied by hand? It would be extremely easy to miss a stroke or add a dot. People in the first century copied in a hurry, and people in the later centuries copied from hand to hand. Today we have a great number of hand-copied manuscripts with some variations in letters.

Hence, God has raised up many who specialize in criticizing the letters of the Bible. They gather many manuscripts and compare them word by word, stroke by stroke. It is a time consuming job, for every letter in the Old and New Testaments has to be verified. Some experts have

* Editor's Note: In reading this section, it must be kept in mind that these messages were given in 1948. However, the principles still retain their value and thus the message has been left in its original form.

traveled to several countries, visiting many museums for the sake of verifying just one letter. Their devotion ought to move us to tears. They are the great scholars of Hebrew and Greek. They spend all their life on such research. How we thank God for raising them up for this difficult task.

Then we have the translators of the Bible. Many people all over the world have spent a great deal of time in carefully translating the Bible. For example, J. N. Darby was used of God to translate the Bible into French, German and English. The popular edition of the Chinese Bible is the combined work of a number of scholars. Sometimes as much as eleven hours were spent on one verse.

Next there are those who write Bible dictionaries. God has raised up many in different countries to study words, animals, plants, beasts and cattle. They have given us Bible dictionaries which greatly help us in understanding. Otherwise how could we know what cedar and hyssop are? Everything in the Bible has been studied, even the difference between a body coat and a cloak. Among the writers of Bible dictionaries are Philip Schaff and William Smith. Schaff's dictionary, written a century ago, is considered one of the best.

Next comes the compilers of concordances. Since the Bible is such a large book, it is not easy for us to find a particular verse: hence the need of a concordance. As a matter of fact, the Bible is the only book that has a concordance. The first concordance ever compiled was Cruden's. Cruden spent many years in compiling his concordance. While undertaking this tremendous task for such a long time, his mind became deranged and the work had to be stopped. However, he resumed the compiling after his recovery six years later. He literally gave his life for the compilation. It is now simple and easy for us to find a principal word in the Bible, but many were the hours spent gathering all the verses in the Bible where that particular word occurs. It required almost a superhuman memory and a prodigious painstaking effort to arrange all the principal words in order. After Cruden, there came Strong's, Young's, and Wiggram's concordances, but all of them are based on Cruden's work. Each concordance has its own specialty and all four are quite reliable.

Following the above compilers are those who do research on Biblical chronology. They scrupulously try to compute the years from the creation of man to Christ. Among these are Archbishop Ussher and Philip Mauro. The wonder of the Bible is that there are scriptural verses which connect without any interruption from the creation of the world to the time of Christ. God has preserved this chronology by giving us a verse here and a verse there. At times it seems as if some verses are missing, yet by diligent searching we can always find the missing links. The years from the creation of Adam to the birth of Christ are like a chain without a break.

Next are the people who study the numerical structure of the Bible. Of these, there are two different schools: one is represented by F. W. Grant, and the other by the Jewish scholars called Massorites. Thirty years ago, a Russian by the name of Ivan Panin also did computation on numerical structure.

It is marvelous to know that each number in Scripture has its particular structure. For example, consider the number twelve: we have twelve tribes, twelve apostles, twelve foundations, twelve months, and twelve fruits. God uses the number twelve with consistency. He intends to manifest His work in that number. Grant in his *Numerical Bible* has opened this up to God's children.

Another school has tried to add up the alphabet of the scriptural words. We know neither Hebrew nor Greek has numerical numbers such as the Arabic 1, 2, 3 and 4. They use their alphabets to represent numbers. Each Hebrew or Greek letter has a numerical value. Ivan Panin, the famous mathematician during the Czarist regime, and his students have added up the letters of all the Bible.

Another school has counted the alphabet in the Old Testament according to paragraphs and verses. This was to help copyists of later generations from making mistakes. For instance, suppose there are 504 letters in a certain paragraph. If the paragraph comes out with 505 letters, it means the copyist has written one word too many. The five books of Moses are made up of 187 chapters, 5845 verses, 63,467 words, and over 300,000 letters. I am not trying to say that such computation has any special value; I simply wish to show young believers how people have spent their time on the Bible.

There is a fourth school represented by Howard Osgood, a most learned person. He spent lots of time studying the Scripture and counted all the Bible words. For example: the total number of words used in the Old Testament is 6417 of which 1798 words are used only once, 728 words are used twice, 448 words are used three times, and 3443 words are used more than three times. In the New Testament, the total number of words used are 4867, of which 1654 words are used once, 654 words twice, 383 words three times, 2176 words used more than three times. The grand total of the words used in the Old and the New Testaments amounts to 11,284 words. That is to say, the Bible in its original language was formed by using these 11,284 words.

Lastly, there are some people who specialize in studying terminologies or emphases in the Bible. For example: Newberry specialized in studying terminologies, Rotherham in studying emphases. We know that in the original Greek every sentence in the Bible has its emphasis. The emphasis in Matthew 5: "Ye have heard that it was said to them of old time . . . but I say unto you," is on the word "I"; that in Matthew 6: "They have received their reward . . . and Thy Father who seeth in secret shall recompense thee," is on "they have" and "Thy Father shall." Rotherham spent his whole life in finding these emphases.

Practical Hints in Studying the Bible

Finally, the Bible must be read daily and consecutively. It is best if the Old and the New Testaments are read together. The reading should not be too fast but rather daily and systematically.

George Muller before his death thanked God for enabling him to read the Bible one hundred times. Young believers should remember the number of times they have read through the Bible. Begin with Matthew in the New Testament and Genesis in the Old Testament, and read through both Testaments. Mark down the number of times in your Bible. We hope every believer will be able to read through one hundred times. If a person lives to be a Christian for fifty years, he should have read the Bible at least twice each year for him to reach one hundred times.

In studying the Bible, two different times should be set apart and two Bibles should be used. The morning time of reading should be accompanied by prayer. It is for the purpose of building up one's own spiritual life. Only three or four verses each morning are enough. Prayers with meditation should be mixed with the reading. The afternoon time is devoted to knowing more of God's word; therefore a longer time may be spent in the reading. This is also the time to find out facts in the Bible. If possible, use two Bibles: one for the morning and one for the afternoon. In the morning Bible, nothing should be written inside except a record of the dates in which one has had special dealings with God while reading a particular passage. The afternoon Bible should record the light received in the reading; hence everything of value can be written in, and circles, straight lines, or colored lines can be drawn all over the pages.

By reading the Word over and over again, gradually our knowledge of the Bible will be increased. If possible, try to memorize one or two verses each day. This may be difficult in the beginning, but it will be a great help later on.

PRAYER

Learning to pray follows studying the Bible. Prayer is both the most profound and the simplest of all Christian exercises. A person newly saved can pray. Yet, many of God's children even on their deathbeds confess that they have not yet mastered the art of prayer.

Answered prayer is one of the basic privileges or rights of a Christian. A Christian is given by God the right of having his prayers heard. If one has been a Christian for three to five years and has not had one prayer answered, his Christian life must be quite questionable. For a child of God not to have his prayers answered is wrong. A Christian's prayers ought to be answered.

"Hitherto have ye asked nothing in my name: ask, and ye shall receive, that your joy may be made full" (John 16:24). He who prays often and has his prayers answered often will be a happy Christian. This is a fundamental experience that every believer must have. One may be careless in other spiritual matters, but in this matter of answered prayer a Christian cannot afford to deceive himself. It is either yes or no. He must seek to have prayers answered.

Ask a new believer if he has prayed today. Ask him if God has heard his prayer, for prayer is not beating the air, nor something done casually. The aim of prayer is its answer. If no answer to the prayer is forthcoming, the prayer is in vain. One must learn to have his prayers answered. Prayer is not just for spiritual devotion; it is also for being heard. If it is solely for devotion, one may pray for hours without expecting any answer. But if prayer is for an answer, then one must pray until the answer comes.

It is therefore imperative for beginners to learn this lesson well so that they may have their prayers answered. It would be a difficult task to correct this foundational lack if one has perhaps been praying three to five years without receiving an answer.

The Conditions for Answered Prayer

A number of conditions for answered prayer may be found in the Bible, but we will pick out a few which we believe are quite sufficient for beginners. These few may well cover over half of the requirements learned by advanced Christians.

1. ASK

To pray one must really ask. "Ye have not, because ye ask not" (Jas. 4:2). "And I say unto you, Ask, and it shall be given you; seek, and ye shall find; knock, and it shall be opened unto you. For every one that asketh receiveth; and he that seeketh findeth; and to him that knocketh it shall be opened" (Lk. 11:9–10).

When I was newly saved, I professed that I prayed daily. One day a sister in the Lord asked me, "Have your prayers been answered by God?" I was surprised because to me prayer was simply praying and nothing more. I prayed but I never thought of whether or not I was heard. Since that time, however, I have prayed to be heard. After she asked me I first examined my prayers to see how many God had answered. I discovered that I had not prayed many prayers of the type that required answers. My prayers were mostly general, so the answers really did not matter too much. It was like asking God for the sun to rise tomorrow; it would rise whether one prayed or not! After having been a Christian for a whole year, I could not find a single instance of answered prayer. Yes, I had knelt before God and uttered many words, but I had not really asked for anything.

"Knock, and it shall be opened unto you," says the Lord. But I had been knocking on the wall! The Lord will not open the wall for you, for He does not know what you really want. If you are truly knocking on the door, He will surely open it for you. If you ask for one thing, the Lord will give that thing to you. Suppose there are several things here: a hymn book, a cup, a Bible, a table cloth and a fountain pen. What do you really want? "Seek," says the Lord. You cannot ask God for a department store; you must ask for something definite.

"Ye have not, because ye ask not." Asking needs to be specific. This is what both seeking and knocking signify. It is seeking for one particular object; it is knocking on the door, not on the wall. Many may pray for a whole week and yet not have asked for a single thing. They do not receive because they have not asked. They have the form of prayer, but they lack the object of asking.

Young Christians should learn how to pray specifically. Do not imitate some brothers who stand and pray in the church for twenty minutes or half an hour but, when asked

85

later what have they prayed for, are at a loss to answer. Many learn to pray long prayers, but yet do not know how to pray for definite things.

Suppose you ask your father or husband or wife or child to get you something. You must tell him or her what it is that you want. Can a doctor go to a pharmacy to obtain a drug without saying what drug he wants? Can one go to the market and not know what to buy? How strange it is for men to come to God's presence without anything definite in mind—just as if anything will do. The difficulty or hindrance to prayer lies in this particular respect. We must ask specifically, not just generally.

Beginners should be clear about this condition of prayer. Otherwise, in times of difficulty they will not be able to pray through. General prayer does not meet a specific need. It may do for ordinary days, but it will not be sufficient when need arises. If our prayer is general in nature, we shall find no help in our hour of need, for then our problems and happenings are all very specific. Only by learning to pray specifically can we have specific experience to meet specific difficulty.

2. Do Not Ask Amiss

Men ought to ask of God. Scripture, however, lays down a second condition: do not ask amiss. "Ye ask, and receive not, because ye ask amiss" (Jas. 4:3). Men may ask God for their needs, but they are not supposed to ask unreasonably or beyond their measure. It requires a few years of learning before anyone can pray so-called "big prayers" before God.

In the early days of our spiritual life, it is rather difficult for us to differentiate between big prayers and praying amiss. It is best for us at the beginning not to ask according to our lusts nor to ask wantonly for what we are not in need of. God will only supply our need and give us that which is necessary. Many times, though, God does grant us exceedingly abundantly above all that we ask. But if the young ask wrongly they will not be heard.

What is meant by asking amiss? It means asking beyond your measure, beyond your need, beyond your actual want. For instance, I have a certain need and I ask God to supply it. I ask according to the amount of my need. If I ask beyond my need, I will be asking amiss. If my need is great, I can ask God to supply that great need. But I should not ask for more, for God has no delight in hearing flippant prayer. Prayer ought to be measured by need; it should not be offered recklessly.

To ask amiss is like a four year old child asking for the moon in heaven. It is far beyond his need. Likewise, young believers should learn to keep their place in prayer. Only after they have more spiritual experience should they pray big prayers. But for now, let them pray within measure. Let them not open their mouths too wide lest they exceed the limit of actual need.

3. Sin Must Be Dealt With

It may be that men have asked and have not asked wrongly, yet still are not heard. Why? Perhaps it is because there is a basic hindrance—sin standing between God and man.

"If I regard iniquity in my heart, The Lord will not hear" (Ps. 66:18). If anyone has a known sin in his heart and his heart clings to it, he shall not be heard. What is meant by regarding iniquity in the heart? It simply means there is a sin which one in his heart will not give up. Though a person may have great weaknesses, God will forgive them. But if one has a sin of which he is aware and yet still desires it in his heart, then it is more than a weakness in outward conduct; it is regarding iniquity in his heart.

The man in Romans 7 is quite different. He declares that what he does is something which he hates. He has failed, but he hates that failure. The man, however, who regards iniquity in his heart is one who will not give up his sin. He neither gives it up in his conduct nor in his heart. The Lord will not hear the prayer of such a person, for sin has hindered his prayer from being answered.

It is important that young believers drive away all iniquities from their heart. Every sin must be confessed and be put under the blood. Though it may not be easy to overcome all one's sins, yet one must not regard iniquity in his heart. God may forgive our weaknesses, but He will not permit us to regard iniquity in our heart. It is of no avail to be outwardly delivered from sin and still be inwardly attached to it. Therefore, young Christians should at the start of their Christian life ask God to be gracious to them that they may be holy in their heart as well as in their conduct. There must be a thorough dealing in the heart for the heart to hate each and every sin and not retain or love or regard one single iniquity. If there is sin in the heart, it is futile to pray because the Lord will not hear.

"He that covereth his transgressions shall not prosper; But whoso confesseth and forsaketh them shall obtain mercy" (Prov. 28:13). Sin must be confessed. After it is confessed, the Lord will forgive and forget. One should go to the Lord saying: "Here is a sin which my heart does regard and finds hard to give up, but now I ask for your forgiveness. I am willing to forsake it; I ask you to deliver me from it that it may not remain with me. I do not want it and I resist it." The Lord will pass over your sin if you so confess before Him. Then your prayer will be heard. This is a matter that should not be overlooked.

4. MUST BELIEVE

There is yet a positive condition that must be fulfilled, and that is, one must believe. Otherwise prayer will not be effectual. The incident in Mark 11:12–24 shows us clearly the necessity of faith in prayer. The Lord with His disciples came out from Bethany. He hungered on the way. Seeing a fig tree afar off, He approached that He might find some figs, but He found nothing except leaves. So He cursed the tree, saying, "No man eat fruit from thee henceforward for ever." The next morning they passed by and saw the fig tree withered away from the roots. The disciples were astonished. And the Lord answered, "Have faith in God. Verily I say unto you, Whosoever shall say unto this mountain, Be thou taken up and cast into the sea; and shall not doubt in his heart, but shall believe that what he saith cometh to pass; he shall have it. Therefore I say unto you, All things whatsoever ye pray and ask for, believe that ye receive them, and ye shall have them."

One must believe when he is praying, because if he believes then he shall receive. What is faith? Faith is believing that he receives what he prays for.

We Christians often have a wrong concept of faith. The Lord says, he who believes that he *receives* shall receive; but we Christians maintain, he who believes that he *will receive* shall have it. Thus we have here two different kinds of faith. The Lord uses the word "receive" twice (Chinese version): once "he receives," then he "shall receive." Many believers, however, fasten their faith to "shall receive." We pray to the Lord, believing that we *shall* receive what we ask. We believe the mountain *will* be removed to the sea. Great seems to be our faith. But we have disassociated faith from "he receives" to he "shall receive." This is not the kind of faith our Lord is talking about. The faith of which Scripture speaks is associated with "he receives." It is far more exact than "shall receive."

I was brought to the Lord through the instrumentality of Miss Dora Yu. Years later she got sick, having cancer of the breast. She heard that I had recently been healed of my tuberculosis. So she wrote and asked me to visit her in Kiang-wan, Shanghai. She thought she showed great faith by saying to me, "I believe God will heal me." I told her that this could not be reckoned as faith, for the Lord Jesus never associates faith with "shall receive." So we had a long conversation that day.

As you know, cancer is a disease which destroys many cells and eats away the flesh. It is most painful and gives off a bad odor. At first the doctor suggested an operation, but later on surgery was useless. Miss Yu, however, maintained that God would heal her. When I tried to show her that merely believing God would heal was not faith, the missionaries who were by her side remonstrated with me and reminded me of Miss Yu's great faith. I answered: "She must believe that God *has* healed her. Only this is faith. It is not believing God *will* heal, rather it is believing God *has* healed. To believe that God will heal or even that God must heal is mere expectation, for faith deals with God's past and present while hope deals with God's future. If I believe God will heal me tomorrow, then I am only *expecting* God to heal me."

Two months later, I received a letter from her. She wrote in her letter, "I have decided today to get out of bed within two or three days, for I believe that God will heal me." As I was rather busy that day and could not visit her at once, I wrote her saying, "First faith, then work. Such work is living. If work precedes faith, it is dead. This is a basic principle. If you believe that you are healed, then your getting out of bed is living; otherwise it is dead."

The next day I hurried to her place. I pleaded with her not to get up. I said to her again: "If you are healed, you can get up; but you cannot get up in order to be healed." She did not get up that day, and she passed away to be with the Lord later on.

So, what is faith? Faith is when you are brought to the place whereby you can claim God has already heard your prayer. It is not when you say God will hear you. You kneel down to pray, and somehow you are able to say: Thank God, He has heard my prayer. Thank God, this is done. Now, this is faith, for it adheres to "he receives." If you rise from your knees and proclaim that you believe God will hear you or God must hear you, however insistent you are, nothing will happen. Your decision does not produce any result.

The Lord says, "Believe that ye receive them, and ye shall have them." He did not say: "Believe that ye will receive them, and ye shall have them." Brethren, do you get the key? True faith knows "it is done" already. Thank God, for He has heard my prayer.

To new believers, permit me to say something out of my experience. Prayer may be divided into two parts: the first part is praying without any promise until the promise is given, praying without God's word to having God's word. All prayers begin this way. Pray by asking God, and keep on asking. In George Muller's case, some prayers were answered in one minute while some were not yet heard even after seven years. This part is the praying part. The second part is praying from the point at which the promise is given to the realization of the promise, from having God's word to the fulfillment of His word. During this period, there should be praise, not prayer. So, the first part is prayer and the second part is praise. Pray in the first part from no word to God's word. Praise in the second part from having the promise till the promise is fulfilled. This is the secret of prayer.

To the people of this world, prayer has only two focal points: I have not, so I pray; after I pray, God gives to me. For example: I prayed yesterday for a watch. After several days, the Lord does give me a watch. This is from nothing to something. But to Christians, there is a third point, a point in between these two: faith. If I pray for a watch and one day am able to claim that God has heard my prayer, then I have reached the point of faith, I know inwardly that I have the watch though my two hands are still empty. A few days later, the watch arrives. Christians need to know how to receive in the spirit; otherwise they have neither faith nor spiritual insight.

Men ought to pray earnestly; they should pray till faith is given. We may say that the first part is praying from no faith to faith; the second part is praising from faith to actual possession. Why should we divide prayer into these two parts? Because once having faith, one can only praise, not pray. If he continues to pray, his faith will be lost. He should use praise to remind God, to speed up the fulfillment. God has already promised to give, what more can he ask? Brothers and sisters all over the world have had such experiences—after faith is given, further prayer is impossible. The one thing to do is to say, "I praise you, Lord." Alas, some brothers do not have this knowledge. God has already promised, yet they keep on praying; and so they pray till they lose everything. This, indeed, is a great loss.

How should one maintain one's faith? By praising the Lord: "O Lord, I praise You, for You have heard my prayer. You heard me a month ago." How precious are the words in Mark 11:24. Nowhere in the New Testament is faith more expressed than in that precious verse. "All things whatsoever ye pray and ask for, believe that ye receive them, and ye shall have them." There are three main points here: (a) pray, with nothing in hand, (b) believe, still with nothing, and (c) believe, and the thing is in hand. May new believers really understand what prayer is and know how great a part prayer plays in their lives.

5. KEEP ON PRAYING

There is another side of prayer which may seem contradictory to what we have just said but which is equally real; it is, men "ought always to pray, and not to faint" (Lk. 18:1). The Lord shows us that some prayers require persistency. We must keep on praying till the Lord is worn out, as it were, by our continual coming. This is not a sign of unbelief, rather it is just another kind of faith, "Nevertheless, when the Son of man cometh, shall he find faith on the earth?" says the Lord. This is the kind of faith which believes that by praying persistently God will eventually answer, with or without a previous promise.

Oftentimes we neither do nor can pray the second time for we have not actually asked for anything. How many of our prayers have we prayed two, three, five or ten times? Many prayers once we offer them are forgotten. Need we wonder that God also forgets them? We can pray and keep on praying only when there is a real need. Then we are under a sort of environment which presses us and moves us to pray. After fifty years have gone by, we may still remember that prayer. O Lord, if you do not act, I will keep on praying.

Such prayer does not conflict with that in Mark 11. Mark tells us that we ought to pray till we are given faith; here it tells us that we ought to pray always and not to faint. Many of our prayers are so without heart that they are soon forgotten by the offerers. How can we expect God to hear such heartless prayers? We ourselves have forgotten and yet we wish God would remember. There is no such a thing. Therefore, young brothers and sisters should learn how to pray and how to pray till they have received what they have asked for.

A certain sister prayed many years for her brother. God did not seem to hear and the situation grew worse. However, one day she declared that she knew her brother would be saved. She looked as if she had great assurance. From where did she get this assurance? It was because she had read the story of the widow pleading with an unjust judge to avenge her of her adversary. She said, "God has shown me that I have never troubled Him enough. Early in the morning I will ask God to save my brother, at noon I will ask again for the salvation of my brother, and in the evening I will remind Him again of the same. If I pray day and night, from dawn to dusk, then one day God will be so worn out by me that He will say, 'All right, I will grant salvation to your brother!' I have determined to pray in this way. Therefore I know my brother will be saved." This sister had really mastered Luke 18:5.

Naturally speaking this sister was a timid person, but now she became exceedingly bold. She troubled God to the extent that God could do nothing but save her brother. After a week her brother was saved! The light she received from the Bible was terrific. What nature could not make of her, light from heaven did; she was transformed into a "violent" person.

Therefore, if you are asking for something, you must learn to trouble God. How can you expect Him to hear you if you yourself have forgotten what you have asked for? If your need is real, you will pray always and faint not. Pray till God *has* to hear you.

Prayer as a Work to Be Done

New believers should take prayer seriously as a job to be done.

First, each one should prepare a prayer-book, a book of prayer accounts. All prayers are to be recorded in this book. Each page should be divided into four items: for example, in my prayer-book of 1948, the first item is the date; the second the subject matter, that which one prays for on a certain date; the third the date of the answer; and the fourth how God answered the prayer. Thus, one is able to know how many things he has asked of God, how many times God has answered his prayers, and how many prayers are still waiting to be heard. In this way one's prayers can be accounted for.

During one year, God answered George Muller's prayers three thousand times. How would he know that figure if he had not recorded them? It is a pity that I threw away my old prayer-books. To look over those old books would be most interesting. Once I was rather ambitious; I wrote down one hundred and forty names in my prayer-book. Eighteen months later, all except two were saved. Some names were entered in the morning and the people saved that very afternoon; others were saved after seven or eight months. Once the things are recorded in the book, they become business items to be seriously transacted before God. There can be no let-up. They must be prayed for over and over again, day by day till the transactions are completed.

The chief advantage of a prayer-book is that it enables one to know how many prayers are answered and how many are not. If our prayers are not heard, not answered, something must be drastically wrong. The old as well as the young should keep a prayer-book. Zealousness alone is futile if prayers are not heard. Unless the way to God is clear, the way to men is blocked. He who is powerless before God is powerless before men. Men ought to seek to have power in prayer before God; otherwise they will be useless persons.

Several matters should be recorded in the book and prayed over daily: (a) All children of God should pray daily for the people of the world that they may be saved. (b) God's children should pray for the full restoration of Israel for they are God's chosen people. Whoever blesses them shall be blessed. (c) Believers should ask the Head of the church to give light, grace, gifts and life to the church. How the church today needs these things. And (d) Christians ought to pray for their countries, that they may lead a tranquil and quiet life in all godliness and purity. These are four big items for which we must pray as well as for other things recorded in our prayer-book.

In using the prayer-book, let it be observed that some subjects in the book need to be prayed over daily, while others may be prayed for once a week. This depends largely on how many things are recorded. If there are not too many, all can be covered by prayer each day. If there are a large number, they can be so arranged that each day of the week certain ones will be covered. I myself for two years set apart each Saturday for a whole day of prayer.

Prayer Has Two Ends

Prayer has two ends: one end is in the person who prays and the other end is the thing or person prayed for. Oftentimes the first end needs to undergo transformation before the other end can be changed. It is futile just to hope for the other end to change. We must learn to pray: "O Lord, where do I need to be changed? Is there yet sin that has not been dealt with? Is there any selfish desire which needs to be purified? Is there any practical lesson of faith that I must learn? Or is there anything that I need to forsake?" If there is need on our side for change, then let it be changed first. Too many of God's children hope the prayed for end may be realized, while they themselves refuse to be changed.

If young brothers and sisters learn the lesson of prayer from the outset as well as learn the lesson of studying the Bible, the church will be greatly strengthened. God will grant a glorious future which will far surpass our past.

LESSON SEVEN

EARLY RISING

Let us get up early to the vineyards; Let us see whether the vine hath budded, And its blossom is open, And the pomegranates are in flower: There will I give thee my love.

S.S. 7:12

Awake up, my glory; awake, psaltery and harp: I myself will awake right early. I will give thanks unto thee, O Lord, among the peoples: I will sing praises unto thee among the nations.

Ps. 57:8–9

Awake, psaltery and harp: I myself will awake right early. I will give thanks unto thee, O Jehovah, among the peoples; And I will sing praises unto thee among the nations.

Ps. 108:2–3

And they gathered it morning by morning, every man according to his eating: and when the sun waxed hot, it melted.

Ex. 16:21

O God, thou art my God; early will I seek thee. My soul thirsteth for thee, my flesh languisheth for thee, In a dry and weary land without water.

Ps. 63:1 (Darby)

When he slew them, then they sought him, and returned and sought early after God.

Ps. 78:34 (Darby)

Oh satisfy us in the morning with thy loving-kindness, That we may rejoice and be glad all our days.

Ps. 90:14

Why Must We Rise Early?

That which we wish to lay before new believers now is extremely simple: we must rise early from our bed each day.

Let me quote the words of Miss Groves, a co-worker of Miss M. E. Barber, who has helped us greatly. She stated that the first choice giving evidence of one's love towards the Lord is the choice between one's bed and the Lord. If one chooses to love his bed more, he sleeps longer; but if he chooses to love his Lord more, he will rise up a little earlier. She spoke these words to me in 1921, but I still sense the freshness of them even today. Yes, a man has to choose between the bed and the Lord. If you love your bed more, sleep on longer; but if you love the Lord more, you must rise up earlier.

Why must we rise early? Because the early morning is the best time to meet the Lord. Other than those few who have organic diseases of the body, all brothers and sisters should be encouraged to rise early. Most of us do not have organic diseases, but are sick only from loving ourselves too much! If the doctors advise us that we have some organic disease such as tuberculosis or heart trouble, then we should not rise up early. We do not want to go to extremes. Those who are sick, we persuade to rest more. But for most, we wish them to rise as early as possible. Dawn is the best time to meet the Lord, the best opportunity to commune with Him.

Many of God's servants in the Bible had the habit of early rising. Manna has to be gathered before the sun rises. Anyone who wishes to eat the food God has promised for him must rise up early. As the sun gets hot the manna melts, and then there will be none. Every young believer needs to know that to receive spiritual nourishment before God, to obtain spiritual food, to be spiritually uplifted and to enjoy spiritual communion, he has to rise up a little earlier. If he rises too late, he will lose his food. The sickly Christian life which prevails among God's children today is less due to any serious spiritual problem than it is to rising up too late in the morning. Do not, therefore, count this a small matter. The spiritual problem of many actually lies in their failure to rise up early in the morning.

It is as if in the early morning before or just as the day begins to dawn, God dispenses His provision of spiritual food and holy communion to His children. Whoever rises late will miss it. Many of God's children do not lack in consecration, zeal and love, and yet they fail to be good Christians because of getting up too late. Rising early has much to do with spiritual life. I have never met a prayer warrior who rises late, nor have I known anyone close to the Lord who gets up late. All who know God at the very least go to God early in the morning.

"As the door turneth upon its hinges, So doth the

sluggard upon his bed" (Prov. 26:14). How does the sluggard act on his bed? He is like a door turning upon its hinges. The slothful person will turn in his bed, but will never leave it. He will turn this way and that way but yet remain in bed. Many people simply cling to their beds. Turning to one side, they find the bed lovely; turning to the other side, they find it still lovely! They love to sleep, to sleep a little longer, and to linger more in bed. Let brothers and sisters notice, however, that if they desire to serve God they must daily rise early.

Whoever purposes before God to rise early will soon experience manifold spiritual profit. His prayer at other times of the day cannot be compared with his early morning prayer. His Bible study at other hours cannot equal that of the morning hour; and his communion with the Lord is never as sweet at other moments as at daybreak. Remember well that the early morning is the best time of the day. We ought to present our best time to God, not to men or to the affairs of the world. He is a fool who spends his whole day in the world and then in the evening, when he is dog-tired, kneels down to pray and read the Bible before retiring to bed. Who can wonder if his prayer, his Bible study and his communion with the Lord are defective? His problem is one of getting up too late in the morning.

Examples of Early Rising in the Bible

God's servants in the Bible were all early risers. Let us note some of them:

1. *Abraham*
And Abraham gat up early in the morning to the place where he had stood before Jehovah.

Gen. 19:27

And Abraham rose up early in the morning . . .

Gen. 21:14

And Abraham rose early in the morning . . .

Gen. 22:3

2. *Jacob*
And Jacob rose up early in the morning . . .

Gen. 28:18

3. *Moses*
And Jehovah said unto Moses, Rise up early in the morning, and stand before Pharaoh . . .

Ex. 8:20

And Jehovah said unto Moses, Rise up early in the morning . . .

Ex. 9:13

And Moses wrote all the words of Jehovah, and rose up early in the morning . . .

Ex. 24:4

. . . and Moses rose up early in the morning, and went up unto mount Sinai . . .

Ex. 34:4

4. *Joshua*
And Joshua rose up early in the morning . . .

Josh. 3:1

And Joshua rose early in the morning . . .

Josh. 6:12

So Joshua rose up early in the morning . . .

Josh. 7:16

And Joshua arose up early in the morning . . .

Josh. 8:10

5. *Gideon*
And it was so; for he rose up early on the morrow . . .

Judg. 6:38

6. *Hannah*
And they rose up in the morning early, and worshipped before Jehovah . . .

1 Sam. 1:19

7. *Samuel*
And Samuel rose early to meet Saul in the morning . . .

1 Sam. 15:12

8. *David*
And David rose up early in the morning . . .

1 Sam. 17:20

9. *Job*
. . . Job sent and sanctified them and rose up early in the morning, and offered burnt-offerings . . .

Job 1:5

10. *The Apostles*
. . . they entered into the temple about daybreak . . .

Acts 5:21

11. *Mary*
Moreover certain women of our company amazed us, having been early at the tomb . . .

Lk. 24:22

Now when he was risen early on the first day of the week, he appeared first to Mary Magdalene . . .

Mk. 16:9

Now on the first day of the week cometh Mary Magdalene early, while it was yet dark, unto the tomb . . .

John 20:1

12. *The Lord Jesus*
And in the morning, a great while before day, he rose up and went out, and departed into a desert place, and there prayed.

Mk. 1:35

These scriptural verses all mention about early rising; it was during this time that many things in relation to God's work and consecration were transacted. God's best servants both in the Old and in the New Testaments were all early risers. They all had the habit of communing with God, dealing with God, and working for God in the early morning. Although we do not find in the Bible any direct command of God to bid us rise early, we nonetheless have sufficient examples of many faithful servants of God who were all early risers.

Therefore new brothers and sisters who wish to follow the Lord must not contemptuously ask, what is the difference between an earlier or a later hour? We have enough experience to convince us that rising an hour late will spoil our Bible study, and rising two hours late will finish our prayer. I personally can testify that though I spend as much time in reading the Bible, yet an hour earlier produces much more than an hour later. Those two hours are not the same. The results in our Bible study and in our prayer are different.

105

Early rising is a great blessing. It is our desire that as he begins his Christian life, not one would miss this blessing of early rising. During the first three years of my Christian life, at least fifty times people asked me how early did I rise. It is such a great blessing, they did not want me to miss it. The world may see no difference in rising two hours earlier or two hours later; such a thing might not make any difference in the things of the world. But let me tell you, in spiritual things, it actually makes a great difference.

Not only were so many of God's servants early risers, even the Lord Jesus Himself rose early. He got up before dawn to pray; He called the twelve disciples early in the day. If we do not rise early enough, we no doubt will become exceedingly poor spiritually.

Besides the twelve Biblical examples mentioned above, we could mention a great number of God's servants through the centuries who were also early risers.

All of whom I have known or read, who have been of some use in God's hand, pay attention to this matter of early rising. They call it morning watch. Have you ever heard of people keeping watch after the sun is up? No, they keep watch until the sun arises. So morning watch must be kept quite early, or otherwise it will not be reckoned as a watch.

Morning watch is truly our Christian heritage; God's children should not throw it away. Even as the church has practiced this morning watch for so many years, so should we maintain and pass it on to the next generation. We will keep the name, calling it morning watch, and exhort the younger generation to rise early in the morning to meet God.

I have known some missionaries greatly used of the

Lord, such as Miss M. E. Barber and Miss Groves. They were both early risers. For many decades, Miss Groves always got up before five in the morning and Miss Barber between four and five in the morning. They told me that they dared not sleep too warmly lest they could not get up in the early morn.

George Muller rose early; so did John Wesley. Many great servants of God got up early. And thus we also expect young brothers and sisters to get up early and not allow time to glide away in sleep.

What to Do After Rising Early

Our aim is not just to get people out of bed in the early morning. We are seeking for spiritual value and spiritual content. So here are a few things which people should do after rising:

1. COMMUNE WITH GOD.

Men rise early in the morning that they may commune with the Lord. "Let us get up early . . . There will I give thee my love" (S.S. 7:12). Being the best time of the day, it should be spent in holding fellowship with God, in waiting quietly before God, in meditating in God's presence, in receiving guidance and impressions from God, and in allowing God to speak to us, our spirits being open to Him.

Communion means having one's spirit opened to God. As the spirit is opened to God, so is one's mind opened. This gives God opportunity to confer light, to supply a word, to grant an impression, and to render a living touch; it also gives the soul the privilege of learning to touch God, to meditate and contemplate, and to draw nigh in heart to God. This, in short, is communion with God.

2. Sing and Praise.

The morning hour is the best hour to sing praises unto the Lord. We may send forth our highest praises at the morning hour.

3. Seek Before God for Food.

This is the time to gather our manna. What is our manna? (Of course, manna points to Christ, but this is not our emphasis here.) It is the Word of God which we daily enjoy and through which we receive strength to walk in the wilderness. Manna is food in the wilderness and has to be collected in the early morning. How can one be satisfied and nourished if he spends the early morning in attending to other affairs?

We have mentioned before that every person should have two Bibles: one to be read at leisure in the afternoon in which many things may be written, and one to be used in the morning in which nothing should be written for it is purely for the gathering of manna. For the morning, do not read long portions; rather open a short passage of the Bible before God and mix prayer with the Word, singing with reading, and communion with the Bible.

We assert that we rise up early for communion. This does not mean that communion is the first step, praise the second step, reading the Bible the third step and prayer the fourth step. Actually it is combining all these, having them mixed together before God. You may appear in God's presence with His Word open before you as suggested in Malachi ("Remember ye the law of Moses my servant, which I commanded unto him in Horeb for all Israel, even statutes and ordinances" Mal. 4:4), or you may join your prayer with the reading of the Word; you may confess your sins after reading God's Word, or you may thank God for specific grace you have received; you may make a special request according to the Word you have read, or you may simply tell the Lord that this particular thing mentioned in the Scripture is just what you lack. To many words, you can say "Lord, I believe"; to many promises you can respond with "Lord, I receive." Sometimes you feel you want to thank the Lord, for His promise is so great; sometimes you are constrained to pray for your brothers and sisters as well as for yourself because you find their condition and yours contrary to what the Bible affirms. No, you are not criticizing or accusing anyone before God; you are merely asking God to fulfill His word in your brethren as well as in you. You, therefore, are confessing both your own sins and the sins of the church. You pray for your own self and for others. You believe on your own behalf and on the behalf of others. You give thanks for both yourself and others.

For this purpose, Bible reading in the early morning should not cover too long a portion. Three to five verses ought to be sufficient for an hour's prayer and communion. Pray and commune with God over everything. There are good examples of this in Nehemiah and David, of how they knew God and knew how to commune with Him.

In the psalms of David, we find he often shifts in the persons he addresses from "you" to "He." At one moment he is talking with men, and at the next moment he has turned it into prayer to God. In the same psalm, he may speak a few words before men and then direct his next words to God. If we do not know how to read the psalms, we will be at a loss to know at what he is aiming. But these very psalms prove that David was one who had communion with God. For myself I cannot speak to the brethren and to God at the same time; yet David's psalms were written with these two mingled.

Such also was Nehemiah. He mixed the managing of earthly affairs with prayer. As he was engaged in his task, he would say a few words and offer a short prayer. Even when he answered the king, he was talking with the Lord as well as with the King. Blending is an important principle in a believer's life.

A similar feature is found in Paul's epistles. For instance, the Letter to the Romans is addressed to the believers in Rome, yet time and again we find Paul's words run to the Lord as if he had quite forgotten the Romans.

Many readers may have read the life of Madame Guyon. Her autobiography has one special feature: whereas most biographies are written for men to read, hers is both for God and for men. In one instant she speaks to LaCombe (for it was LaCombe who bid her write her autobiography); at the next she talks with the Lord. This is what we call communion. Where it begins and where it ends are indefinite. As soon as one's spirit rises up, he or she goes forth to meet the Lord. It is not necessary to lay down the affairs of the world in order to pray, nor to take them up only after prayer is finished.

Indeed, early in the morning is the best time to gather manna. Learn to blend prayer and praise and communion into the Word of God. For a while you are on the earth and in the next moment in heaven; you are in your own presence for a second and then move on to God's presence the next instant. In so spending your time each morning before God, you will be daily satisfied. You will have fed on the Word of Christ, for Christ is the Word of God. You will also have allowed the Word of Christ to dwell in you richly. This way of reading the Word of God, of feeding on the manna, is indispensable. To the many weak brothers and sisters staggering in the wilderness, we would like to ask whether they have eaten. They cannot run because what they have eaten is not sufficient to nourish them. Manna must be gathered in the early morning; therefore get up a little earlier lest you miss your food.

Let there be communion, praise, manna and prayer in the early morning. "O God, thou art my God; early will I seek thee" (Ps. 63:1 Darby). "And returned and sought early after God" (Ps. 78:34 Darby). In both psalms we find the word "early" in the original. Early in the morning is the time for prayer. After having communed with God and fed on manna, one is strengthened to lay all things before God and to carefully pray over them. It takes strength to pray; the weak cannot pray. With the new strength gathered from communion and from feeding on the manna, one is able to pray—for himself, for the church and for the whole world.

So every new believer needs to know the four things he ought to attentively do before God each morning: communion, praise, Bible reading and prayer. If he neglects these four, the day will declare it. Even a person like George Muller confessed that whether or not he was fully fed before God in the morning determined his spiritual condition for the whole day. His early morning foretold the day. Many Christians find their days hard because their mornings are ill spent. (I acknowledge that a person would not be easily affected by outward circumstances if he knew the separation of spirit and soul and thus the consumption of the outward man. This, however, is a totally different aspect.) To new believers, the exhortation must be directed towards early rising, for once they become careless about this, they will be careless about almost everything. The difference it makes in the day is exceedingly great, whether one has had nourishment in the morning or has gone hungry.

I remember a well-known pianist once remarked: "If I

do not practice for one day, I notice something wrong; if I do not practice for two days, my wife notices something wrong; and if I do not practice for three days, the whole world notices something wrong." Let us not forget that if we fail to have a good morning with the Lord, not only ourselves and our wives but the whole world will surely know it. Why? Because we have failed to reach the source of our spiritual life. Young believers ought to discipline themselves very strictly and get up early in the morning to practice communion, praise, Bible reading and prayer before God that thus they may be well nourished.

Things to Be Observed in Early Rising

Finally, we would like to mention a few things which are related to the practice of early rising:

a) To rise early, one needs to go to sleep early. All early risers have the habit of going to bed early. It is improper to expect to retire late and rise up early. That would be like burning the candle on both ends.

b) Do not set too high a standard for rising early. Some decide to rise up at three or four o'clock in the morning. They try it for a few days and quit. Trying to rise too early will end up in failure. Let us rather take a moderate course—say, around five and six o'clock, just before or at the dawning of the day. If the time is set too early, it will be difficult to sustain. To set too high a standard will produce a bad conscience and we need to maintain a conscience without offence. Thus we do not advocate extremes. Let us each consider the matter carefully before God, taking into consideration the physical and environmental conditions of our lives, and then set a standard for ourselves as to what is the appropriate time for us to rise.

c) Cultivate the habit of early rising. It is inevitable that one will meet some difficulty in the first few days of early rising. He will love his bed and find it hard to climb out. It takes some time to establish a habit. In the beginning one has to force oneself to rise, but after a while he can get up early without effort.

Human nerves are like the tree on the hilltop that bends in the direction of the wind. If it is blown always in one direction, it develops the habit of leaning in that direction. Suppose you have the habit of rising late. It is like having your nerve bent northward. But after you try to rise up early many times, your nerve will begin to turn its direction southward. Then, instead of it being difficult to get up early, you will find it hard to get up late, for you cannot sleep any longer! Until that habit is formed, though, ask God to give you grace that this good habit of early rising may be developed. Try it many times; do it again and again. Daily learn to desert your bed and get up early until you have formed the habit of rising early to enjoy the grace of morning communion with God.

d) Our sleep should not exceed eight hours. Pardon me for bypassing physicians in speaking directly to new believers. I think few people need more than eight hours of sleep. Do not make yourself an exception. Unless your doctor prescribes more rest because of some organic disease, eight hours is quite sufficient for the ordinary person. Do not worry about your health in rising early. Many love themselves too much and worry themselves to ill-health. The average need for an ordinary person is six to eight hours of sleep. So long as you keep to the average, you will have enough rest.

e) The sluggard needs a little push. We are now in the

Church, being members of the Body of Christ. How, then, can we be careless? The sluggard among us needs a little pushing, a little pulling, a little shaking. Likewise, those who sleep only three or four hours need a little correction too, for the lack of rest may become the cause of sickness. The average is eight hours; too much is unnecessary, too little is insufficient.

Give Help to the Young Believers

I hope that those who are more advanced in the Lord and have some weight before God will take up the responsibility of maintaining the practice of morning watch in the church. They themselves should both rise early and should help the young into this blessed state. Whenever there is opportunity, they should ask the young: "Brother, at what time do you get up these days?" Many rise up at eight, eat breakfast in five minutes and then have five minutes to hurry through the Bible. They spend too much time in bed. So older ones in the Lord should inquire of the younger ones, perhaps continuing such inquiry for as long as a year.

Remember: early rising is the first habit a Christian ought to form. Gathering on the Lord's Day is also a habit. The young ought to form both these habits, but the responsibility for helping them is with the older believers. How very many have never enjoyed the blessing of early rising!

If the church makes progress in this exercise, if many brothers and sisters learn to rise early, if each one goes to God and receives a little more light each day, how rich the whole church will become and how full of light she will be. If the church is poor it is only because too few are receiving anything from the Head. Should we learn to receive from the Head, even though each one of us receives only a little, the result will be that the church will become exceedingly rich.

Our way lies not in having ten or a hundred special workers or ministers to labor among us. We expect all the members of the Body to rise up before God to receive riches and grace. If all the brothers and sisters go this way, the riches among us will be without measure. I often think what we are able to give to the brethren must be far inferior to what God could give. But what each member does receive from the Head is for the gain of the whole Body May there be many, many such receptive vessels before God, each one gaining his little portion to share with the Body. Therefore, let us not despise early rising as a small thing. Let us all keep the morning watch, and then we shall all together advance one more stcp.

TITLES YOU
WILL WANT TO HAVE

by Watchman Nee

Basic Lesson Series
Volume 1—A Living Sacrifice
Volume 2—The Good Confession
Volume 3—Assembling Together
Volume 4—Not I, But Christ
Volume 5—Do All to the Glory of God
Volume 6—Love One Another

The Church and the Work
Volume 1—Assembly Life
Volume 2—Rethinking the Work
Volume 3—Church Affairs

The Better Covenant
A Balanced Christian Life
The Mystery of Creation
The Messenger of the Cross
Full of Grace and Truth—Volume 1
Full of Grace and Truth—Volume 2
The Spirit of Wisdom and Revelation
Whom Shall I Send?
The Testimony of God
The Salvation of the Soul
The King and the Kingdom of Heaven
The Body of Christ: A Reality
Let Us Pray
God's Plan and the Overcomers
The Glory of His Life
"Come, Lord Jesus"
Practical Issues of This Life
Gospel Dialogue
God's Work
Ye Search the Scriptures
The Prayer Ministry of the Church
Christ the Sum of All Spiritual Things
Spiritual Knowledge
The Latent Power of the Soul
Spiritual Authority
The Ministry of God's Word
Spiritual Reality or Obsession
The Spiritual Man

by Stephen Kaung

Discipled to Christ
The Splendor of His Ways
Seeing the Lord's End in Job
The Songs of Degrees
Meditations on Fifteen Psalms

ORDER FROM:

Christian Fellowship Publishers, Inc.
11515 Allecingie Parkway
Richmond, Virginia 23235